THE STORY

Annie Oakley

By EDMUND COLLIER

Illustrated by LEON GREGORI

ENID LAMONTE MEADOWCROFT
Supervising Editor

PUBLISHERS Grosset & Dunlap NEW YORK

© EDMUND COLLIER 1956

To

WALTER HAVIGHURST

Another Friend of Annie Oakley

PRINTED IN THE UNITED STATES OF AMERICA

LIBRARY OF CONGRESS CATALOG CARD NO. 56-7344

The Story of Annie Oakley

*She rode standing up on
a galloping white horse*

THE STORY OF
Annie Oakley

Contents

CONTENTS

[*vi*]

Illustrations

[*vii*]

ILLUSTRATIONS

THE STORY OF
Annie Oakley

CHAPTER ONE

"I Can Go Hunting"

Mother, tell us about the time Daddy rescued you."

Kept indoors by the threat of storm, six-year-old Annie Moses was restless. She wanted a story.

Her older sister, Sarah Ellen, looked up from the deer hide she was working to softness in a tub. "You've heard that a hundred times," she said. "Don't bother Mother now."

The door of the log cabin swung open. The cold fall wind blew across the floor. It swirled the ashes on the hearth. Mary Jane and Lyda came in carrying a log four feet long. Elizabeth rushed to shut the heavy door. The girls dropped the log on the fire, and Annie turned to watch the sparks fly up the great chimney.

[*3*]

It was a big family for such a small cabin—
four girls older than Annie; John, two years
younger; and Hulda, the baby.

Annie's mother was sitting in a hide-bottom
rocking chair, mending clothes. Annie leaned
on her arm.

"Please, Mother!" she begged.

Susan Moses looked down thoughtfully into
the little girl's clear gray eyes. She smiled and
stroked Annie's chestnut hair. "Thee loves
that story, doesn't thee, Annie?"

"Yes, Mother."

"Well, so do I, so I'll tell it to thee again."

Annie's mother and father were of the
Quaker religion. They always said "thee" and
"thy" for "you" and "your."

Little John was playing with some chips of
wood near the fire. Two-year-old Hulda was
watching him. At the promise of a story, John
left his play and hurried over. Hulda trotted
after him.

The three children clustered so closely
around their mother that she could not sew.
She put her work in her lap and began.

"It was back in Pennsylvania. My mother
died when I was very young. My father married again. Then he died and my stepmother

married again. My new father was very cruel. He made me work from morning to night. And he beat me."

"Why didn't your stepmother stop him?" Annie interrupted. "I would have stopped him. I would have taken you away."

"Well, my stepmother could not do that," her mother said. "And thou art too young to understand why. Be still now—if thee wants to hear the rest."

Annie pouted, but held her tongue. A gust of wind rattled snow against the windowpanes. Her mother looked up anxiously.

"Thy father is late," she said. "I wish he were at home."

The older girls were bringing in more logs.

"Pile up plenty," their mother told them. "By morning we may have to dig our way out to the woodpile."

"Go on, Mother," Annie commanded.

"One day, my stepfather was about to whip me for some work I had not done to please him. But he had hardly begun, when a man on a fine white horse came by the farm. He heard me cry out, and came galloping into the yard. He snatched the whip away, and warned my stepfather he must never touch me again.

[5]

"This man had settled not very far off. Later he found out that my stepfather had whipped me again. This time he came over and did not stop to talk. He took me up on the back of his horse and carried me away—"

"Just like a knight . . ." Annie said, her eyes shining.

"Just like a knight," Mrs. Moses agreed.

"And what happened then?"

"He left me with friends till I was older, and then he married me."

"How long did you have to wait?"

"Not long, Annie. Only till I was fifteen. By then your father owned an inn on the main road from Pennsylvania to Ohio. People moving West in covered wagons passed the inn, and many stopped there. We did well."

"Why did you leave?" Annie asked.

"One night a guest overturned an oil lamp and set the inn on fire. The inn burned down and all the money we had saved burned with it. We had no money to start again, so we joined the pioneers going West. We hoped that we could find free land in Ohio and live by farming. So we settled here in Darke County, near Greenville."

"Just like a knight," Annie said

"Was it long ago?"

"Long for you, Annie. Four years before you were born. But it doesn't seem long to me."

"Tell us—" Annie began—for she never had her fill of stories—but her mother stopped her.

"Enough for now—it's your suppertime."

Mrs. Moses put her sewing in its basket and got up. Annie went to the window and put her nose against it. The pane was icy cold. The snow fell with a whisper in the dim light. Annie stood there watching the drifts pile up. She wondered how her father would ever get home.

But soon her mother called out, "Supper's ready."

The children sat on benches that ran the whole length of the table. Their one-dish supper of ponade was simple but good. It was made of bread cut into small squares and mixed with plenty of maple sugar. Boiling water poured over it melted the sugar and made the ponade nice and hot. Cream poured on top made it rich.

The hungry children gobbled it down almost as fast as their mother could ladle it out.

Soon not a scrap was left, and they were fighting to lick the pot.

After supper their mother put the two younger ones to bed. Annie was an independent child. She could shift for herself.

Her mother said, while she was tucking in Hulda and John, " 'Tis a bitter cold night, Annie. Use all the spare covers thee can find or thee will freeze."

Annie found a buffalo robe and dragged it over her blankets. She climbed into the snug bed and lay there sleepily. The buffalo robe was heavy, but warm. She pulled it up around her neck, and the coarse, curly hair tickled her chin.

She could hear the wind whistling around the chimney and driving the snow against the windows. Off in the woods it made a steady roar through the treetops. Swaying branches squeaked as they rubbed together. And deep in the forest a frozen trunk burst with a sharp crack.

Annie knew her mother was worried about her father. That morning he had loaded his wagon with corn and wheat and set out for the mill, fourteen miles away. He planned to have his grain ground into flour and meal, to exchange some of this at the crossroads store for coffee and sugar, and to be home before dark.

"But it's very dark now," Annie told her-

self. "Perhaps something has happened."

As she lay awake thinking about her father, she heard her mother tell Sarah Ellen to leave

his place set at the table. She heard the older
girls putting more logs of wood on the fire. It
crackled and blazed up. Annie could see the
shadows of the flames playing on the wall
through the bedroom door. They were keep-
ing a big fire going.

After a while Annie dozed off, but what
with the noise of the storm, the crackling fire,
and worry over her father, she did not sleep
soundly.

Once she woke up and heard her mother
praying for her father's safe return. She slept
again. Then she woke up from a dream to hear
trace chains rattling outside the door. A horse
coughed above the wind.

"Thank God he's back!" her mother cried
softly.

Annie heard her take down the big plank
bar that held the door shut. She felt the icy
draft as the door swung open.

"Jacob!" There was alarm in her mother's
voice.

Annie slipped to the floor and pattered out
barefoot into the wind-swept room. Her older
sisters were already at the door. Her father
was sitting stiffly on the seat of the wagon. He
had tied the ends of the reins together and

[*11*]

hung them around his neck. He could not guide the horses. But they had found their own way home through the blinding snow.

"Bring an armchair with a blanket," Mrs. Moses said tensely as she hurried out into the storm.

Sarah Ellen threw a buffalo robe over a stout chair. She and Elizabeth carried it out, and set it beside the front of the wagon. Mary Jane climbed up and took the reins from her father's neck. Then she and her mother, struggling with the weight, eased Mr. Moses into the chair. Annie watched from the door as her mother and three older sisters carried her father into the house.

His legs were like logs and his fingers were curled tightly shut. How he had managed to stay on the wagon seat was a miracle. He shivered a little as they set the chair down in front of the fire.

Mary Jane and her mother helped him to the bed and tried to rub some life into the stiff limbs.

Lyda and Sarah Ellen unhitched the horses and led them through the drifts to the shelter of the shed. Then the girls carried the supplies into the house.

No one paid any attention to Annie. She stood shivering in her bare feet, watching by her father's bed. At last her mother noticed her. She patted her head and said, "Go to bed now, Annie. You'll catch cold. One sick person is enough to care for."

Back under her buffalo robe Annie lay awake a long time. She could hear her father tossing and moaning. She wondered what would happen to her and the rest of the family if he did not get well.

Next morning she was wakened by the sound her older sisters made, throwing a big log on the fire. The smell of fat bacon and steaming oatmeal were good to her nostrils. She lay there comfortably a minute. And then she remembered her father.

She dressed quietly and went out into the main room. The door to her father and mother's room was closed. Her mother, at the fireplace, wearily brushed back a lock of hair from her forehead. She swung out the crane with the black kettle of oatmeal. Annie thought she must have been up all night.

"How is Daddy?" Annie asked.

"He is not well, child . . . Sit up now and have thy breakfast."

[*13*]

Sarah Ellen and Elizabeth were dressing John and Hulda on a bench by the fire. The children wriggled away and ran to the table.

While their mother ladled out the oatmeal, Mary Jane dished up the bacon. Lyda uncovered a Dutch oven that sat on the coals. In it were brown-topped biscuits. With milk for the oatmeal and blackstrap molasses for the biscuits, it was quite a feast.

But Mrs. Moses was too tired to eat. She helped Hulda with her oatmeal and then watched the others.

"Children," she said at last. "Thy father is a very sick man. It may be many months before he can take care of the farm or earn any money. We will all have to buckle down now and work hard."

"Perhaps Sarah Ellen and I can find jobs with some of the neighbors," Mary Jane offered.

"Perhaps thee can," her mother said. "And I might get some nursing to do in Greenville. I have done that before. It is lucky I have so many fine girls. For someone must be here to take care of the babies and look after thy father."

"Elizabeth and I will do that," Lyda said

[*14*]

Annie gave another good look at the long rifle

quickly. "Don't you worry about it, Mother."

There was a silence while each of the girls thought what she could do to help. Little Annie was staring at her father's big gun that hung over the mantelpiece. Suddenly she broke the silence.

"I can go hunting," she said brightly. "I'll help get food."

The whole family looked at her. Then her sisters burst out laughing.

"What would you hunt with?" Lyda asked.

"Daddy's gun," Annie said seriously. "I've watched him use it."

"Well, it would knock you right into the next county, if you ever shot it off!" Elizabeth exclaimed. And they all laughed again.

Annie didn't think that what she had said was very funny. But she gave another good look at the long rifle. She saw she could hardly lift it, let alone hit anything with it. And then she laughed too.

It was an anxious winter for the Moses family. Though Mrs. Moses and the older girls got jobs whenever they could, there were times when food was scarce. Poor Mr. Moses was never well enough to leave his bed. Steadily he grew worse, and in March he died.

CHAPTER TWO

Traps

LITTLE Johnny Moses sat up in his trundle bed.

"I'm awful hungry, Annie," he said softly. "I feel all empty inside."

"Well, lie down and go to sleep again," Annie whispered. "When it's time to get up, Mother will have something for you to eat."

Annie was hungry too, but she was eight now—too old to complain.

Two years had passed since her father's death. They had been hard years for all the Moses family. Mrs. Moses had been forced at last to give up the farm and even to sell Old Pink, the milk cow.

Luckily a neighbor had lent the family an abandoned log cabin to live in, but there was

[*17*]

never enough money to buy the things which were needed and seldom enough food.

"It will soon be winter again, too," Annie thought. "Then we'll hear the wolves howling in the forest the way we did last year."

She shivered and pulled her blanket closer. All at once she heard her mother's voice just outside the cabin. She climbed out of bed and went to the window. Her mother was kneeling not far aff, praying, looking toward the rising sun: "O God, I know Thou art with us; I need bread and meat to feed my children but I know Thou wilt not desert us. Amen."

Annie crept back into bed. "Poor Mother's so worried," she said to herself. "I wish I knew some way to help her." She snuggled under the covers and lay still, thinking. At last she had an idea.

Later that morning, after Mrs. Moses had left for work, Annie called John and started off for the woods.

"What are we going to do?" her little brother asked.

"You'll see," was all Annie would tell him.

They came to a brush patch near a fenced-in cornfield. It was a wonderful place for quail. The corn had been harvested and the stalks were stacked in rows, like little wigwams up and down the field.

"Help me drag some cornstalks into the brush patch," Annie told John.

"What for?" he asked.

"We're going to make a trap," Annie said as she crawled under the fence and reached for some cornstalks.

"A trap?"

"Yes. To catch quail. We need more food, Johnny. Here, grab these stalks."

Annie had heard her father tell how he had made a trap when he was a boy. She hoped she could remember.

With flat sticks the children dug a sloping trench. They built a cabin of crossed cornstalks over it. They sprinkled kernels from an old ear of corn along the trench for bait. They propped the front of the trap up on a stick. Annie hoped that a quail would knock down the stick. Then the trap would fall and he'd be caught.

When the trap was all set, Annie piled brush thickly all around it. For there were raccoons, muskrats, and even 'possums that would be glad of a meal of quail. The brush would help to keep them away.

[*19*]

The children finished the trap and sat down some distance off to watch. But suddenly Annie realized she was starving. She had been too interested in her work to think of it before. She glanced at the sun.

It was past noon. "Come on, Johnny," she said as she got up, "it's past lunchtime. Don't you dare tell anyone what we've been doing. I want the quail to be a surprise."

With Johnny behind her she ran home and burst into the cabin, breathless with excitement from her project as well as from running.

Her sisters had finished lunch.

"Where in the world have you been?" Sarah Ellen asked.

"And where's Johnny?" Elizabeth added.

"Coming," Annie said, as she slid onto a bench at the table.

"Wash before you eat," Sarah Ellen told her. "What have you been up to? You're covered with dirt."

Before Annie could answer, Johnny came panting across the clearing, and through the door.

Behind her sister's back Annie put her finger to her lips.

"Wash up, Johnny," she said.

They went outside to the pail and wash basin on the bench by the door. They doused themselves with water, wiped their faces on a coarse huck towel, and sat down to a meal of boiled squash and beans. Vegetables had been their principal food for most of the summer. Annie's mouth watered as she wondered if there would be meat that night for supper.

It was the middle of the afternoon by the time she and Johnny got away again. Sarah Ellen was in the garden picking late shell beans. But she was leaning over with her back turned to them. The children sneaked through the worm fence, and slipped off into the woods.

The sun was halfway down the sky when they came in sight of their trap. The air was crisp and cool, and the woods were striped with the long, slanting shadows of afternoon.

"Nothing came," Johnny said.

He was right. The front of the trap was still up. Annie felt very discouraged.

Johnny started down for a closer look. But Annie put out a hand and stopped him. Her keen eyes had seen a movement in the brush.

"Quiet!" she whispered.

They heard a little chuckle. Then a small,

gray-brown head poked out from the brush, and a quail stepped cautiously toward the trap. It walked forward to investigate. It found the first kernel of corn—pecked it up.

"Bob-white! Bob-white!" it sang. Another quail appeared behind it. The two birds were fat as pumpkins.

Annie gripped Johnny's shoulder tight to keep him quiet. Her heart was thumping. The

first quail poked its head into the trench. It moved halfway under the front of the trap. It was going in, eating as it went. Annie hoped the bird wouldn't trip the trap until the sec-

ond one got in. Luck held. The second bird had just got its tail out of sight when the door to the cornstalk cabin dropped. The birds were trapped.

Annie let go of Johnny's shoulder and sat down suddenly. What a relief!

It was almost dark when the two children approached the cabin. Their mother had come home. She was at the fireplace stirring corn meal mush in a big iron kettle which hung from a crane over the fire. She didn't hear the door open quietly. But as she swung the crane out, she saw the children and her eyes widened in surprise. Each child was grinning broadly, and each carried a plump quail hanging head down.

"Where didst thou get those?" she asked.

"Trapped them," little Annie said proudly.

"We made the trap," Johnny announced.

Susan shook her head. "My babies—trapping!"

By this time the older girls had clustered around, examining the quails.

Elizabeth asked, "How did you kill them?"

"Lifted the trap a little," Annie said, "and when they poked their heads out, we hit them with a stick."

[24]

Mrs. Moses stared at her. "I wouldn't have believed thee could do it! Where didst thou learn how?"

"Father used to tell us how he trapped when he was a boy," Annie said.

"So he did. And thou remembered it. Thou'rt a clever little girl, Annie."

Annie tried not to look too pleased with herself.

"Now we'll have meat, Mother," she announced soberly.

"And the Lord knows we need it. All right, girls. Pluck and clean the quail. We will have them for supper."

CHAPTER THREE

Annie Gets a Gun

ALL THAT fall Annie spent trapping. With little John scrambling after her she explored the fence rows and thickets for the best place to set traps. The family had meat to eat, and they were stronger for it.

Even so, there were many nights when the children went to bed hungry. Finally Mrs. Moses decided that she must send little Hulda away for a while, to live with friends.

"But I don't want her to go away," Annie protested. "Why must she?"

"Because there will be one less mouth to feed," her mother replied.

Annie glanced at the long rifle which hung over the fireplace. "If you'd let me try, I could use Father's rifle," she said. "I'd shoot squirrels and rabbits and maybe even a deer. Then there would be meat enough for everyone."

"No." Her mother spoke firmly. "Thou art too small to handle anything so dangerous. Thee must not touch that gun."

"Then let Sarah Ellen or Lyda try."

"Not me," said Sarah Ellen. "I'm afraid of guns."

"And I couldn't hit a barn if I was inside it," Lyda said.

So little Hulda was sent away, and the long rifle remained on the hooks over the fireplace. It fascinated Annie. Her father had been a good shot. Annie had often watched him load and clean the gun. She remembered that he had always tried to shoot small game through the head.

"Why spoil the meat?" he said. "When I was a boy we used to consider it a disgrace to hit a squirrel anywhere but in the eye."

One day Annie's mother and Mary Jane were away at their jobs and the older girls were off cutting firewood for the winter. Eight-year-old Annie was at home taking care of Johnny. She was leaning against a porch post, soaking up the last warmth of the fall sun.

Her younger brother was building a hut of
sticks in front of the cabin. Squirrels were
busily collecting nuts from the hickory trees
that grew beyond the clearing.

One big squirrel scampered along the rail
fence about fifty yards away. It sat up with a
nut in its paws and scolded at Annie. It tore
the outer shell off the nut with its long, sharp
teeth and scolded some more. Johnny ran out
and threw stones at it. The squirrel twitched
its tail angrily and ran up and down the fence.
Then it sat up stiffly and began to scold again.

Annie watched it, thinking longingly of hot
squirrel pie. Suddenly she stood up, called
quietly to Johnny, and slipped into the cabin.
By the time Johnny joined her, she had
dragged a bench over to the hearth, and was
trying to get the long gun that still hung on
hooks above the mantel.

"Johnny! I can't reach it. Hold the bench
steady for a minute."

Johnny steadied the bench. Annie climbed
up on the mantelpiece. It was a narrow perch
and Johnny watched wide-eyed, fearing she
would fall. Annie lifted the butt of the long
rifle from its hook, and slid it down to him.

Next she got powderhorn, bullets, caps, and

patches. She stood on the bench. While Johnny held the gun upright, she loaded it just as she had often watched her father load it—but she poured in a little too much powder.

Then she jumped from the bench, lifted the heavy gun, and clutching it tightly, she crossed the cabin and went outside. The big squirrel was still sitting on the fence, busy with his nut.

Carefully Annie laid the barrel of the long rifle over the porch railing. She glanced behind her to see where Johnny was, and motioned him to stay back.

Kneeling down, she snuggled the butt of her father's rifle to her cheek. His words flashed through her mind: ". . . a disgrace to hit a squirrel anywhere but in the eye."

No squirrel keeps still for long. The second Annie saw the head of this one in the gun sights, her right hand squeezed tight around the throat of the rifle. At once there was a great roar and a burst of black smoke. Annie toppled over backwards. When she got up the squirrel had disappeared and Johnny was running across the clearing. He reached through the fence row, picked up the squirrel, and came running back carrying it by the tail.

While Johnny held the gun upright she loaded it

Annie was rubbing her nose as he approached. He pointed at the squirrel's head, almost as proudly as if he'd shot the animal himself.

"Right through the eye, Annie!" he said. Then he glanced up. "Wow! Look at your nose!"

Annie didn't know whether to laugh or cry. She felt a little sick. Because she had held the gun too loosely, it had jumped and the butt had banged her nose. She felt of it gingerly. It was sore and swollen. And she was beginning to worry now about what her mother would say.

Together she and Johnny got the gun back on its hooks. Annie laid the squirrel on a shelf, and settled down to wait for her mother's return.

It was dusk when her mother got home. Annie didn't mention the squirrel right away. She was waiting to get up her courage.

In the struggle with the bench some ashes had been pulled out of the fireplace onto the hearth. Mrs. Moses spied them. She reached for her broom, and began to sweep them back into the fireplace. Annie was watching her. She knew she should have done this herself. As

[*31*]

the ashes settled on the hot embers, suddenly there was a sparkling sputter.

Her mother stopped sweeping and stared at the fire.

She swept in more ashes. More sparkles! She stopped sweeping again. She leaned on the broom, and gave Annie a long look.

"Who's been playing with gunpowder?" she asked sternly.

Johnny said nothing. Annie took a deep breath.

"We—" she began. "I mean I—"

"Annie! What happened to your nose?"

Mrs. Moses looked up over the mantel. The rifle was just as it had been. She looked back at Annie.

"Hast thou been shooting that gun?"

"Yes, Mother—I—"

Her mother spoke gravely. "But I told thee not to. I didn't think—"

Annie caught her mother by the hand and led her to a shelf where she had laid the squirrel.

"Mother," she said, "you know quail are getting scarce near by. If you let me use the gun, I can get more squirrels, and rabbits, and wild turkeys, all sorts of things."

[32]

Mrs. Moses sat down on the bench by the table. She drew her daughter to her. "Thou art so small, Annie, for such a long rifle. If—"

At this point the other girls came in from the woods. They saw the squirrel at once.

"Who brought that?" Elizabeth asked.

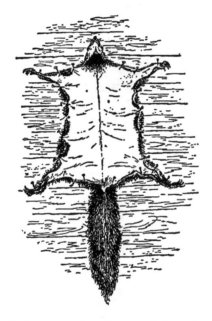

Little Johnny piped up. "Annie shot it—through the head."

The two older girls looked at her in surprise.

"Did you, honest?" Elizabeth asked.

Her mother answered before Annie could

[*33*]

speak. "Yes, she did," she said proudly. "How she ever got that gun down and aimed it, I don't know."

Looking down at Annie, she smiled. "Next time thee mustn't spill gunpowder on the hearth. Thee might set the cabin afire. And Annie—be careful."

Annie took this for permission to use the long rifle whenever she pleased. She made hooks to hang the gun where she could reach it. From then on she was the family huntress.

CHAPTER FOUR
The Wild Cow

THAT autumn and into the winter, eight-year-old Annie spent most of her time hunting. She rigged up a sling so that she could carry the rifle across her back. Tramping through the woods and over the hills with the heavy gun, she became strong as a young wild-cat.

She found that she was naturally a good shot. With practice she was getting better.

She wore a heavy woolen skirt, thick woolen jacket, long black stockings and a flat hat. Her ankle-high laced boots weren't much protection from the cold and wet. But she greased them carefully to make them as waterproof as possible.

All their clothes were homemade, and the older girls did much of that. Annie was good with her hands and learned to knit well.

But she had not yet learned to read. On Sunday mornings her mother would read aloud from the Bible. To Annie and the others many of the stories were quite exciting.

In the evenings the children would roast chestnuts over the open fire, while their mother told stories of her early life in Pennsylvania.

Yet with all that, Annie and Johnny found time to play. They made snowmen and built snow forts. Then they would persuade the older girls to be an attacking army, with snowballs for ammunition.

That winter closed in like the last. The game went far away to escape Annie's deadly gun. The snowdrifts became so deep that she could not follow their tracks. As the winter drew to an end provisions got lower and lower. Sometimes there was nothing to eat but flour and water gravy poured on homemade bread.

At last the snow began to melt. Annie was able to get out and find a few winter-thinned rabbits and squirrels. Everyone looked forward longingly to the spring when there would be dandelion greens, brakes, and other wild things to freshen the dreary meals.

Mud time came when the roads were quagmires at noon and froze hard again at night. One morning just after daybreak, Annie thought she heard the rumble of wheels coming along the lumpy, still frozen road.

She jumped out of bed and ran to the door, pulled out the bar and swung it open. No one was in sight. But she listened. Clear as could be, the rattle of wagon wheels came through the bare trees in the early morning stillness.

"Someone's coming!" she shouted. "Get up! Someone's coming!"

She dashed for her clothes. There was an excited bustle and stir in the cabin as the others answered her call.

By the time Annie was dressed, a wagon had pulled into the yard. A big, hump-shouldered man with a great brown mustache, and a wide mouth, was on the seat.

"Anyone home?" he shouted cheerfully.

Annie knew him. He was a farmer named Dan Brumbaugh who lived a few miles away. He had recently lost his wife. A pile of something in the wagon box was covered with a piece of canvas.

Mrs. Moses appeared at the door—and all the girls behind her.

"Mornin', Susan," Mr. Brumbaugh said. "Thought I'd drop by and see how you wintered."

"We came through, Dan. But with no extra flesh—as thou can'st see."

It was clear enough that she and the children clustered behind her were pretty thin.

"And how didst thou winter, Dan?"

"Well enough, Susan. But with my wife gone and the children married and away, it's more than lonesome."

Dan got out of the wagon and threw back the canvas.

"One thing," he said, "I've got more food than I know what to do with. I brought over a few things I couldn't use."

Annie ran eagerly forward. There were several bags of flour and meal in the wagon. Dan pulled a ham and a side of bacon out from under the seat, and started for the house.

" 'Tis good of thee," Susan said, a catch in her voice. "Come in, Dan, and I'll cook up some of that sidemeat, and make some mush from the meal. Thee must stay and eat with us."

"Don't mind if I do," Dan said. "I'm surely tired of my own cooking."

"Corn meal mush! Hasty pudding!" Annie loved it. But it would be even better with milk. They hadn't had any all winter. Annie had a sudden inspiration. She would be helpful. She would get milk, and perhaps impress Mr. Brumbaugh. She ran inside, grabbed a lard pail, and ran out again. No one noticed her in the general excitement.

During the winter, a stray black cow had come in and hung around the place. It had lived on scraps of old root vegetables and some two-year-old hay that was in the barn. It was so lean and wild that no one had thought much about it. But Annie had noticed that with the coming of spring it was beginning to give down a little milk.

"I'll do it," thought Annie, "and we'll have milk for breakfast." She had learned to milk Old Pink, the cow that they had had before. But Old Pink had been gentle as a kitten.

The black cow was standing in the shed with her head in the manger, lapping up a few wisps of straw. Annie crouched down on the cow's right side, grasped the lard pail between her knees, and started to milk. The old cow

[39]

lifted her head out of the manger, looked at Annie, and mooed as though annoyed.

Annie paid no attention. She had got half a cup of milk, when the cow shifted restlessly. Annie followed her up.

"Her side's against the wall now," Annie thought. "She can't move any farther that way."

But Blackie had made up her mind. She didn't want to be milked. She lifted her right foot, and stuck it right in the pail. Annie fell over backwards. The cow lowered her sharp, short horns and went after her. Annie scrambled to her feet and dodged behind an old grindstone in one corner. Blackie pawed and bellowed and hooked at the grindstone. At any second she might knock it over and stick one of those sharp horns between Annie's ribs before the girl could escape.

Annie didn't want to call for help. But she was tempted to, when suddenly Dan Brumbaugh appeared. Behind him were Annie's mother and sisters and her brother.

Dan had a big stick in his hand. He poked Blackie with it. The angry cow turned and went for him. But Dan hit her a clip on her sensitive nose, and she thought better of it.

*Blackie pawed and bellowed and hooked
at the grindstone*

She galloped out of the shed and started to nibble willow shoots—pretending that she didn't really care.

"What in the world art thou up to?" Annie's mother asked.

"I was trying to milk the cow. I thought we'd have milk on our mush," Annie explained.

Mrs. Moses looked at her soberly and shook her head. "Thou art such a tomboy. Always trying to do a man's work. Sometimes I wonder thee aren't killed."

Dan Brumbaugh laughed and slapped Annie on the back. "You're a great girl," he said. "But you're too little to manage everything all alone."

He put his hand on Annie's shoulder and started her toward the house. "Come on, folks, I'm starved," he said.

Annie thought it was good to have a strong, confident man around. The mush was ready when they got back. One of the girls fried some ham and bacon. To celebrate Dan Brumbaugh's visit they used up the last of their maple syrup on the mush.

When Dan drove off, saying he'd be back soon, the whole family felt the weight of the long, sad winter lifted from them. The children were happier than they had been for many months. As for Mrs. Moses, there was a look of peace on her face, as if she had made up her mind about something. Soon she and Dan Brumbaugh were married and the family moved to his place. It was still a log cabin. But it was a bigger and better one than Annie had ever lived in, and there was a nice little farm around it. Also Dan's cow was not wild and gave plenty of milk.

CHAPTER FIVE

First Job

I<small>T</small> WAS a beautiful summer afternoon. Annie was ten years old. She and her mother were sitting on the front steps of Dan Brumbaugh's cabin.

Only a few months before, another baby sister had been born. They had named her Emily. Their mother was feeding the baby. Annie was knitting a pair of socks for her.

Robins were singing in the treetops. A black-and-orange oriole was swinging in his nest at the tip of an elm branch.

Out front, the vegetable garden was fresh and green. In a field beyond it, the broad leaves of the new corn were more than knee high.

FIRST JOB

Chickens scratched in the barnyard to the right. A red-and-green rooster flapped up onto the fence, and crowed lustily. Beyond the barnyard, the brook where the stock drank was sparkling in the sun.

Through the woods Annie heard the sound of light wheels. She turned her head. A buggy drawn by a young black horse was coming into the clearing. A tall, bony woman was driving.

Annie jumped up with pleasure. It was Mrs. Eddington, a great friend of the family. She and her husband ran the County Home where old people, poor people, and orphans with no families of their own were cared for.

Annie's mother beamed with pleasure as the buggy pulled up in front of them. They didn't have many visitors.

"Sally Eddington!" she said. "Light down and visit. Annie, take Mrs. Eddington's horse to the stable."

When Annie came back from putting up the horse, Mrs. Eddington and her mother were talking busily. Annie picked up her knitting.

Mrs. Eddington watched closely. Annie's deft fingers worked quickly. The stitches were tight and even.

[45]

The tall, gaunt woman looked surprised.

"Annie knits real good for a ten-year-old girl," she said. "I wish I had you to help at the Home, Annie. I would teach you to sew."

Annie's eyes brightened. "On your sewing machine?" she asked. "I'd like that. Can I go, Mother?"

"Now, Annie, thou art too fast with thy tongue. Mrs. Eddington hasn't asked thee even."

"But I would, in a minute, if I thought you could spare her," Mrs. Eddington said. "She could play with my Frank, who is almost her age, and help take care of my baby."

"Please let me, Mother! Please!" Annie begged.

Her mother thought a minute. "There are many hands to help in this house," she said finally. "I could spare Annie if thou really wants her. There's no doubt she wants to go."

Annie jumped up and threw her arms around her mother. Her ball of yarn flew in one direction, her half-knitted sock in another. As she picked them up, her mother said to Mrs. Eddington, "Tha'll stay to supper, won't thee? It will give us a little time to get used to the idea."

"I don't know as I should," Mrs. Eddington objected. "I told my husband I didn't know when I'd be back, but—"

"Then it's settled. We'll have chicken and fresh peas to celebrate. Annie, wilt thou pick some peas?"

Annie grabbed a basket and hurried to the garden. Her heart was beating with excitement. This would be the first time she'd ever spent a night away from a little log cabin. The Eddingtons had a real house, big barns full of hay to slide in, and a fresh running creek with a pool for swimming. Her mind reeled with plans as her skillful fingers twisted off the full-podded peas.

She piled the basket full and brought them back. Then Annie and Mrs. Brumbaugh and Mrs. Eddington sat on stumps in front of the cabin, shelling them. Mrs. Brumbaugh glanced up at the afternoon sun.

"Wonder where Dan is," she said anxiously. "He said he'd be home in time to kill a chicken for supper."

"Where did he go, Susan?" Mrs. Eddington asked.

"A fox got into the hen yard last night and made off with his best layer. It's not the first time. Dan grabbed his gun and took off, mad as hops."

"When a man goes hunting, there's no telling when he'll be back," Mrs. Eddington remarked.

"Thee don't know Dan," said Mrs. Brumbaugh. "He's always home when he says he'll be. If he'd not been sure, he'd have said so."

She shelled the last pea in the basket and stood up. "I'll kill the chicken myself," she added. "Annie, go get the cows."

This was Annie's regular chore, and she liked it. She ran to the barn and slipped a

halter on the black mare. Then she climbed
to the mare's back and dug her bare heels into
the animal's plump ribs. The mare grunted
and made off at a slow gallop.

Annie found the two cows and their calves
mooing at the pasture gate. She let down the
bars and they streamed past her.

"This is pretty tame," Annie thought. She
wanted to make the cows run, but she didn't
dare. They might get nervous and refuse to
give down their milk. And then would she get
a scolding! But one of the calves was dawdling
behind. Suddenly Annie slid off the black
mare's back. She grabbed the lagging calf by
the tail, gave a yell and a twist. The calf
bawled and made off in fright to its mother.
Annie hung onto its tail, and came sliding into
the barnyard on her heels, in a cloud of dust.

Her mother was coming out of the barn
with the chicken she had just killed and
plucked.

"Annie!" she said. "Wilt thou never be a
lady?"

Before Annie could answer, a wagon came
into the yard. Two neighboring farmers were
on the seat. One climbed down and came toward Mrs. Brumbaugh.

"Dan got hurt. We brought him home," he said.

"Is he hurt badly?" Mrs. Brumbaugh asked quickly. "What happened?"

"He took a short cut coming home, over the railroad bridge," the farmer said. "A train came along, and he had to run to get across. I reckon he stumbled. Anyway, he fell off the bridge."

Susan Brumbaugh gasped. Thrusting the chicken at Annie, she hurried to the tailgate of the wagon box. Dan was lying in the wagon on his back, his eyes closed.

"Dan. How are you?" she asked.

Dan opened his eyes. His face twisted with a spasm of pain. Then he answered, "Just bunged up a bit, I guess. I'll be all right, Susan. . . . It was lucky that our friends came along."

The men carried Dan gently into the cabin, and laid him on the bed. "We'll go for the doctor," one told her.

Supper that night wasn't the happy meal the family had been looking forward to. Susan Brumbaugh hardly sat down.

When the doctor came he said Dan had a broken leg, a badly bumped head, and probably other injuries. He gave him something to ease the pain, and set the leg. That was all he could do. Dan was in for a long siege in bed.

When the doctor had gone, Mrs. Eddington asked Mrs. Brumbaugh, "Don't you want Annie to stay here at home with you now?"

"No," said Annie's mother, "we can get along all right. The child has her heart set on going. And she has earned a little pleasure."

"But I'll stay and help you if you need me," Annie told her mother. "I could go some other time."

"No. We can manage. Dan wouldn't want you to give up this visit on his account."

"And perhaps you can earn a little money at the Home," Mrs. Eddington put in. "The county will pay you if you can make good dresses for the children there. You could help your mother that way."

"Then I'll go," Annie decided promptly. And she scrambled up the ladder to the loft to get her clothes.

CHAPTER SIX

Sulphur and Wild Honey

IT TOOK Annie no time to pack as she had little to take. Johnny brought Mrs. Eddington's horse from the stable, and Annie helped hitch it to the buggy. Then she climbed up beside Mrs. Eddington. They drove off to a chorus of good-bys, and warnings to Annie to be good and take care of herself.

It was almost dark, but a rising half-moon soon cast a dim light through the woods. Annie was too excited to be sleepy. This was her first visit away from her family. Though it was long past her bedtime when the buildings of the County Home came in sight, she was wide awake.

[52]

Softened by moonlight, the buildings had a friendly look. The Eddingtons' own low white house was set among shade trees. The plain board dormitory where the poor people lived stood a little distance off. Between them were a huge barn, chickenhouses, wagon sheds, a corn crib, and the springhouse. A pretty creek winding among them gurgled sleepily, as Annie jumped down from the buggy.

Annie drew a deep breath filled with the smell of new-mown hay.

"I'm going to like it here," she thought.

A man came from the barn and led away the horse and buggy. Annie and Mrs. Eddington tiptoed into the house so as not to wake anyone up.

Next morning Annie came downstairs to the smell of frying bacon and baking johnnycake. She followed the smell to a big kitchen with a cast-iron woodstove in the corner.

The Eddington girl, Sally, was setting the long table in the middle of the room. It was covered with a red-checked tablecloth, and plates filled with all sorts of jellies, pickles, cheese, and doughnuts.

Mrs. Eddington, at the stove, said, "Sally, this is Annie Moses. She's come for a visit."

Sally was quite a little older than Annie, but very friendly.

The girls started chattering away when a great clatter sounded on the stairs. A pair of shoes came tumbling down into the hall, followed by a boy with tousled black hair.

"Frank, you go back up and brush your hair and put on your shoes. We've got company," Mrs. Eddington scolded. "This is Annie Moses."

Frank cast a glance at Annie, but said nothing. "Perhaps he doesn't like girls," Annie thought.

Whatever he thought, Frank was to find Annie as good a playmate as any boy. She was still small for her age, but she was square-shouldered, open-eyed, and sure of herself. Frank was bigger. But even so, he soon learned that Annie would more often be leading than following in any game they played.

Breakfast was ready in a few minutes. All through the meal Annie's eyes kept straying to the sewing machine in the next room. Her coarse clothes made her feel a little uncomfortable. As she ate the last of her doughnut she decided to make herself a colored gingham dress like Sally Eddington's, if she could get the cloth and Mrs. Eddington would show her how to do it.

Right after breakfast she went in to the other room and began examining the machine.

"It's broken," Mrs. Eddington told her. "I've got to get the man to come out from town and fix it."

Annie was disappointed and showed it. Mrs. Eddington smiled. "The very next time someone drives to town to do an errand, I'll send him a message," she said. "But we may have to wait a long time before he comes. Meanwhile we can cut and baste some dresses."

Annie had hardly heard Mrs. Eddington's words. Already she had lifted up the metal plate under the needle, and looked inside. Lint was all tangled up in there.

"I think I can fix this," she said.

Mrs. Eddington shook her head. "It takes an expert an hour or two to put a machine like that in shape," she said as she returned to the kitchen.

Annie studied the machine thoughtfully for a few minutes. Then she went to work. She took the machine all apart, and carefully cleaned and oiled each part. Next time Mrs.

[55]

"I think I can fix this," Annie said

Eddington walked through the room she saw the parts lying on top of the machine.

"Mercy, child!" she said in a startled voice. "I hope you're not ruining that machine completely."

"I'm not," Annie said. "I'm *fixing* it." She began to put all the clean parts together. Everything fitted. Nothing was left over. She put a piece of cloth in the machine and began to stitch. The machine worked perfectly.

Mrs. Eddington was delighted.

"My land, child!" she exclaimed. "I can hardly believe it. You certainly are good with your hands. I'm going to give you two dollars. The County would have to pay more than that to have a man do the job."

Annie was so happy that if she'd been at home she would have turned handsprings.

This was the first money she had ever earned. She planned to give it to her mother when she went home. With Dan Brumbaugh laid up, her mother would need every cent she could get, and in those days two dollars would go a long way. To Annie it was a fortune.

For a while Annie was happy at the County Home and had a fine time playing with the

Eddington children. But the hard luck that seemed to follow the Moses family hit again. Annie came down with scarlet fever!

It spoiled a good part of her summer. But when it was over Mrs. Eddington decided that Annie should stay on for the winter and go to school with her children.

Though Annie's mother hated to be parted from any of her big brood, she felt this was best for her daughter, and gave her consent. Annie had a fine winter. She not only went to school and began to learn to read, but she did many things to help around the Home.

She learned to make clothes for the old women and orphan children, and she thought up ways of making the clothes more attractive, such as sewing red bindings on collars and pockets. Mrs. Eddington was so pleased that she gave Annie some pretty red gingham to make the dress that she wanted.

Though she missed her family, the winter was a pleasant one for Annie. So was the following spring. One Saturday when there was no school she and Frank Eddington went for a ramble in the Darke County fields and woods. Fresh shoots of bright green skunk cabbage showed along the stream borders. Dogwood

trees were just coming into bloom. Meadow-
larks in the fence rows overflowed with song.
High twigs swayed as chattering squirrels
chased each other through the treetops. Cow-
bells tinkled on milk cows walking to water in
the curve of the creek. From far away floated
the soft call of a turtle dove, followed by the
low echo of its mate.

Much as Annie liked school, the woods were
her deepest love. But at ten the pangs of hunger are strong. Before the sun was straight
above them, the two children were headed for
home and some dinner.

In front of the Eddingtons' house was a pair
of well-groomed horses, hitched to a bright
black buggy with red wheels.

"Wonder who that is?" Annie said.

"Someone rich—from the buggy," Billy
guessed.

Spring medicine—sulphur, cream of tartar,
and wild honey—was cooking on the stove.
Always Annie would connect that smell with
the man who stood in the kitchen. He was tall,
clean-shaven, dressed in store clothes. He gave
Annie a glance that sized her up.

Mrs. Eddington said, "Annie, this gentleman wants to hire one of the orphans to live

[59]

with his family and take care of their baby.
I'm very busy. Will you take him around the
Home so he can talk to some of the girls?"

Annie nodded. Her mind was working
quickly. She and Mrs. Eddington had talked
about her going to work for a family. Mrs. Ed-

dington thought it might be better for her than living at the County Home. And Annie wanted to earn more money than she could make with her sewing. Perhaps this was her chance.

She was never bashful, and as she took the man from one girl to another, she asked questions.

"What will the girl have to do?"

"Mostly keep my wife company," the man told her. "Take care of the baby some. Help a little with the housework now and then."

"What will the pay be?" asked Annie.

"Fifty cents a week. Really a gift. It would be like living at home and getting paid for it. The girl will go to school. We'll pay for her books. And we'll keep her clothed."

"Do you live in town?"

"Near by, but we have a big farm, one of the best in the county."

Then the man began asking Annie questions. She told him about her hunting, and how eager she was to go to school.

He said, "The woods near our place are full of game. Any girl we hired could go to school and hunt all she wanted to besides."

Finally the man said, "I can't make up my

"What will the pay be?" Annie asked

mind about any of these girls. Let's go back to Mrs. Eddington."

He stayed to dinner and they talked some more.

At last he put his hand on Annie's shoulder. "This little girl right here is the one I want, he said. "She's the brightest, most capable girl you have."

"We know that," Mrs. Eddington said quietly. "How do you feel about it, Annie? Would you like to go?"

Annie's eyes were shining. "Oh, yes," she said, "I want to go! I hoped I'd be asked."

"If the gentleman can wait for a few days, I will write to your mother and see what she thinks about it."

The man said, "I can wait, if it's not too long."

CHAPTER SEVEN

Wolves

O NE DAY two weeks later Annie was standing impatiently in the Eddingtons' kitchen. Her eyes were glued to the window. Beside her was her small bundle of clothes. She was wearing the new gingham dress she had made from the cloth she had been given.

Behind her, Mrs. Eddington was ironing.

"What if he doesn't come? It's getting late," Annie said anxiously.

"Then you'll just stay here. Does it matter so much, Annie?" Mrs. Eddington asked.

"I'll be sorry to leave you. But I do want to go," Annie said.

Her mother had given her consent. Mrs. Eddington had written to the man and he had replied that he would come that day around noon to get Annie.

She had said good-by to Frank and the Eddington girls when they left for school in the morning. If the man didn't come soon, they would be back, and she would have to say good-by all over again. She'd been ready since dinner at twelve, and now it was almost four o'clock.

For days Annie had lived in dreams of her new job. What fun it would be to live near a town and go to school there! On week ends she would hunt in the woods near the great farm, and bring home meat for the table. And all the time she would be earning money.

But now she was feeling sadder and sadder. She was about to give up and put on her old clothes again when she heard the crack of a whip.

Wheels rattled over the little bridge across the creek. The shiny buggy came in sight. The tall man pulled up the horses sharply in front of the house. They were sweating and breathing hard. The back of the buggy was full of packages.

Annie had the door open almost before the horses stopped. Mrs. Eddington was right behind her. Seeing them there, the man waved his whip and shouted, "Sorry I'm late. I won't get out. Got to get home soon as I can. Are you ready?"

"All ready," Annie cried, her heart beating fast.

She went back for her bundle.

Mrs. Eddington put her arms around her, and held her tight.

"We're sorry to lose you, Annie," she said. "Come back any time you want to."

"Thanks. I won't forget," Annie said.

She gave Mrs. Eddington a last kiss and climbed into the buggy.

She was hardly settled in the seat when the man cracked the whip and was off.

Before they got out of sight, Annie looked back and waved at Mrs. Eddington, who was still standing in the doorway.

The man didn't explain why he was late. But that didn't bother Annie. With his black derby hat, ruddy face, and long mustache, he looked as handsome as ever. He smelled of tobacco, but Annie rather liked that. It reminded her of Dan Brumbaugh. As the horses trotted briskly along she felt quite important, though a little lonesome.

As the horses trotted along she felt quite important

She tried to make conversation, but the man had little to say. For some time they rode along in silence. Then he pointed with his whip to a single light far down the road.

"There it is," he said. "Home."

He pulled the horses up at last before a small board house, which was hardly more than a shack.

"Go on in," he said. "I'll put up the team."

Annie's heart sank as she climbed down from the buggy and opened the door. There was only one room, cut in two by a curtain that was pulled halfway back. In one corner a baby lay sleeping on the double bed.

In another corner a dark, dull-eyed woman was at the stove. She turned as Annie came in.

"You're the new girl, I guess," she said in a crowlike voice. "Take your things upstairs right away and then come down for supper."

Annie crawled up a flight of steep narrow stairs to a windowless, tiny room under the eaves. She put her bundle on the narrow bed and felt of it. It was just boards covered with a thin straw tick.

There was no light in the room except what came dimly up the stairs. Annie looked around. The only other furniture was an old packing box that she supposed was meant for a table.

She heard the man come in to the room below her. He spoke crossly to his wife.

"Where's the girl?"

"Upstairs," the woman said shortly.

"Get her down. She can put supper on," he ordered gruffly.

Annie shuddered as she hung her blue jacket on a nail.

"Those two are like wolves," she thought.

Ever after she called them "the Wolves." That's what she called them in the life story she wrote later. No one knows their real names.

From then on Annie's life was work without rest. She got up at four o'clock to cook breakfast. And it was a big one. Ham or bacon that Annie had to slice, fried mush, fried potatoes, and biscuits. When breakfast was over Annie had to feed the stock and milk the cows. Then the dishes must be washed. After that she had to rock the baby to sleep.

Then it was time to start getting dinner. First Annie had to go to the garden and pick vegetables. Then she had to get them ready. After dinner more dishes, more baby care. Then came the evening chores in barn and

house. And when supper was over there was
often mending to do.

All summer Annie did the best she could.
She hoped that in the fall when school started
there would be some relief. School began. She
saw children going by the house while she was
carrying skim milk to the hogs. They had their

books and slates and lunches
under their arms. Sometimes they waved to her.

"When am I going to school?" Annie would
ask.

"Later," the woman would say. "When the
fall work is done and my husband has more
time for the chores."

Annie, of course, could not yet read or write
very much. In the few months she had gone to
school at the Eddingtons' she had made only
a beginning. The Wolves wrote home for her.
They read letters to her that they said her
mother had written in reply. Actually these

were all made up to make Annie think her mother was glad Annie was working, and that the money she earned was a great help. The letters they sent to Annie's mother said that Annie was very happy and was going to school and wanted to stay.

Finally Mrs. Wolf invited a friend to visit her and wanted Annie out of the way. So she sent her to school. Annie went without lunch or books or slate, and her clothes were poor and thin and patched. Because she had learned so little, she had to study with children much younger than herself.

Perhaps shame made Annie more proud than she should have been. Perhaps she showed off in an attempt to pretend she didn't care about her poverty and lack of schooling. Whatever the reason, in the cruel way children sometimes have, they teased her. They made up a song about her that went something like this:

"Moses poses! Moses poses!
No one knows where she got her clotheses.
She hasn't a rag to blow her nose with.
Moses poses! Moses poses! Moses poses!
Moses poses!"

Moses poses! For years those words would sometimes ring in Annie's ears. She was so hurt that she never liked her last name again, and later changed it to something else. Some of the children soon would have stopped teasing her. But she never had time to find this out. For in two weeks Mrs. Wolf took her out of school again.

The winter wore on and another summer passed. Slappings and pinchings, even whippings, were added to overwork. By the time the next winter came around Annie was almost worn out. She didn't think she could stand it much longer.

But the Wolves kept reading to her fake letters from her mother, saying how glad she was that Annie was still working, and how much she needed money. So Annie said nothing about leaving.

One cold night, after a hard day, Annie sat in the kitchen trying to darn stockings. But she just couldn't keep her eyes open, and fell asleep. When Mrs. Wolf found her nodding over her work, she flew into a rage. She hit Annie so hard that the girl fell out of the chair.

"Why, you lazy little witch!" the woman shouted. "Get out of here." Then she pulled

Annie to her feet, pushed her out into the snow, and locked the door.

Mr. Wolf was away at a meeting. When he reached home, he found Annie shaking in the cold and let her in. That night she was sick and cried out in her sleep. The Wolves shook her awake to quiet her.

Now Annie felt she could stand no more. Next morning after breakfast she said to Mrs. Wolf, "Won't you please take me home? I'm too tired to work here any lŏnger."

"But your mother wants you to stay with us," Mrs. Wolf said, giving her a shove toward the dishpan. "She writes in every letter that she needs the fifty cents you are earning."

It was forty miles home. Annie hadn't even a penny. She thought someone must soon come to rescue her. But her mother thought she was happy. Annie wished she could read those letters. Perhaps they were just a pack of lies.

In the spring the Wolves went visiting. They left Annie with orders about a vast amount of work to be done while they were gone.

"If you do well, my husband will take you

home for a visit when we get back," Mrs. Wolf
told Annie.

Annie took good care of the stock and the
house and garden. When the Wolves returned
they seemed pleased, though they gave no
praise, and Mrs. Wolf said nothing about the
vacation she had promised Annie. So next
morning Annie got up her courage and asked,
"When may I go home?"

Mrs. Wolf turned on her with a twisted
grin. "Don't you dare ask to go home!" she
shouted.

"But you promised—"

"I just wanted to make sure everything
would be taken care of while we were away."
Mrs. Wolf grinned again.

That night before Annie went to sleep, her
mind was made up. She would run away the
first chance she got.

CHAPTER EIGHT

Runaway

A WEEK later the Wolves went to spend a day with relatives. They left Annie a huge basket of clothes to iron.

When they said they would be gone all day, a flush of excitement swept through her. She hoped they didn't notice her cheeks turn red.

Before they left, she started ironing hard. Mr. Wolf brought the buggy to the door. As Mrs. Wolf went out she turned to Annie and said, "See those clothes are all finished when we get back."

Annie said nothing. She kept on ironing without looking up, for fear Mrs. Wolf would read her purpose in her eyes.

The horses' hoofbeats faded down the road.

Annie looked out the window and watched the buggy disappear. Then she turned back to her ironing. Suppose the Wolves had forgotten something and should come back!

She forced herself to iron for half an hour. Then she put the iron on the back of the stove, and turned down the drafts. She was sure that this was the time to go. She might not have another chance for months.

Her legs shaking, she climbed the steep stairs. Quickly she tied her few things in a bundle. She crept downstairs, opened the door, and stepped outside. The garden and the animals were there as usual. But how different Annie felt!

For a minute she stood still, wondering about her bundle. Someone, seeing it, might know she was running away and stop her. But she couldn't afford to leave it.

She grasped it tightly and started walking toward the village. She had a strange feeling that someone was following her. She wanted to run. But she held herself back.

She had almost reached the railroad station when someone called, "Stop, Annie! Where are you going?"

Annie stiffened in fear. Then she smiled.

[77]

The voice belonged to Kate Darle, a girl who had shared her lunch with Annie at school.

"I'm going home," Annie told her excitedly. "I'm running away."

"Really?" Kate asked, wide-eyed. "Aren't you scared?"

"I'm scared stiff." Annie said.

"I'm glad you're going," Kate said.

"Kate, Annie—"

It was Kate's mother calling them from the porch. When Annie told her what she was doing, Mrs. Darle said, "It is the best thing, Annie. People have been worried about you, child, but no one dared interfere."

She put up a lunch for Annie and gave her train fare. Then she and Kate walked with Annie to the station. They stood on the platform and waved good-by as the train moved off.

Annie sat down beside a kindly looking old gentleman, who saw at once that she was frightened. Reaching into his carpetbag, he brought out a striped stick of candy and gave it to Annie.

"Thanks," she said, with a quick smile.

Annie was starved for sweets. She ate some of the candy.

"Where do you live?" the old man asked.

"Near Woodland," Annie told him.

"You'll have to get off at Dawn, won't you, and walk quite a way? And how old are you?"

"Twelve."

The old gentleman shook his head. He wondered why so young a girl was traveling alone.

He seemed so kind that Annie told him just what she was doing and why.

"I hope my mother won't be angry," she said.

"I'm sure she won't. It's too bad you couldn't get away sooner. I don't believe your mother ever got any of your messages, or had any idea what the place was like."

It was late afternoon when Annie got off the train at Dawn and started for home. It was dark when she reached Dan Brumbaugh's place. Annie pushed open the door. The woman who turned from her dishes was not her mother. But Annie knew her—a Mrs. Clark.

Mrs. Clark looked startled when she saw who was standing on her doorstep. "Annie Moses!" she exclaimed. "Where did you drop from?"

Annie explained as quickly as she could.

"Why, you poor child," the woman said. "No need for you to walk all that way home in the dark. You just come in and spend the night."

Anxious as Annie was to get home, she was tired and glad enough to accept the invitation.

Mrs. Clark told her news that her mother no doubt had written her long ago, but that

the Wolves had kept from her. Dan Brumbaugh had never recovered from his injuries.
He had been dead for over a year. Annie's
mother was married again to a much older
man, a Mr. Shaw. Annie's older sisters had all
married and moved away. The Clarks had
bought the Brumbaugh place.

Annie sank to sleep that night in a bed
that was blissfully comfortable. Next morning she thanked Mrs. Clark for the night's
lodging.

"I'm glad of the chance to do something for
one of your mother's children," Mrs. Clark
told her. "She's done plenty for me."

It was ten miles to Mr. Shaw's farm. Annie
made the dust fly. When she came into the
yard, her mother was hanging out clothes.
She didn't see Annie until Annie called,
"Mother!"

Then she turned.

"Annie!" she said, almost unbelievingly,
and rushed to gather the girl in her arms.

At last she held her daughter off at arm's
length.

"Thou hast grown up, Annie," she said.
"And thou art so thin. Have they treated thee
badly?"

Annie nodded. Tears were streaming down

[*81*]

"Annie!" she said, almost unbelievingly

her cheeks. She brushed them away hastily.

"They were cruel," she said. "And they lied to me. But it doesn't matter, now that I'm home."

Then there was a clatter of hoofs. The younger children came riding into the yard. John was on a smoky colt. Emily had a real riding horse, and Hulda was on a fat young heifer.

"Annie! Annie!" they cried. Jumping from their mounts, they surrounded their older sister, and all began asking questions at once.

Annie had to have all the news. The three animals were gifts from Grandpap Shaw, as they called him.

Annie missed Dan Brumbaugh. He had been a good stepfather. But when Grandpap Shaw got home that night, Annie knew she would like him, too.

He was quite an old man, tall, thin, with a stringy, droopy mustache. His eyes were not very strong. But he was kind and gentle.

"Annie, I'm glad you're back," he said warmly. "We've worried about you."

When Annie told him her story, he was terribly angry. Next morning he set out to try to get the Wolves arrested. But there were few laws then to protect children. There was nothing he could do.

Grandpap Shaw had been well off. But he had lost his farm and most of his money. When Annie got back the family was about to move again.

Grandpap put what little money he had left into a piece of land near the village of North Star. Friends and neighbors pitched in to help build a log cabin.

Annie's sister, Lyda, and her husband, Joe Stein, came out from Cincinnati to be in on the fun. Joe was a carpenter and a great help in building the cabin.

Once again Annie had a new home. But there was a three hundred-dollar mortgage on it that would have to be paid. Everyone would have to pitch in and work. It looked as though Annie still would have to put off going to school.

CHAPTER NINE

A Letter from Lyda

IT WAS a beautiful morning, and Annie
let the barefooted roan horse make his own
pace. Elderberries were ripe along the road-
side, their purple overlaid with dust from
passing wagon. wheels. Sweet-smelling fox
grapes climbed high into the trees. Lazy, winding creeks showed good spots for muskrat
traps. Farmers were busy getting in the last of
their corn crops, and wild apples were drop-
ping along the crooked fence rows.

Annie had spent a wonderful summer,
hunting, eating, soaking up sunshine. In spite
of the exercise she got roaming the woods of
Darke County, she had put on weight.

This fall morning, she felt full of life and

very happy. She lovingly touched the gun hung across the front of her saddle. It had served her well.

Annie shifted the basket of game she had slung across her shoulder. The roan pricked up his ears, and looked down the road, toward the curve ahead. As they rounded it, a strange figure stepped from a dark walnut grove into

the road. He was tall and gangly, dressed in deer-hide clothes and a coonskin cap. He led a horse as lean and bony as himself. The horse was piled high with a bale of pelts lashed to the saddle.

Annie knew who the man was—old Coonskin Brown. He lived by himself somewhere
in the back country and came to town when he
got enough skins to trade.

"Hi, Mr. Brown," Annie said as she caught
up with him.

Coonskin squinted up at her from under his
shaggy eyebrows.

"Been't you one of the Moses girls?" he
asked.

"Yes, sir," Annie said respectfully, though
she could smell the old trapper a mile off. She
slid off the roan and walked beside him.

"That's right," he remembered, "you're
the little one, Annie, ain't it?"

"Yes, sir. How's trapping?"

"Not like it used to be. I git a few skins."

"Do you make much money?" Annie asked.

"Not so's to git rich, young 'un. I eat, and
keep myself in tobaccer."

That's all Annie could get out of the old
man about his business. There were rumors
that he had stacks of money hidden away. But
he certainly didn't look it.

Coonskin began asking the questions.

"Goin' shoppin' in Greenville?"

"Got to get Grandpap's horse shod before

[*87*]

fall plowing, and get my gun fixed," Annie told him.

"Did it give out on yuh?" Coonskin drawled.

"It just needs a new spring. When Frenchy La Motte puts one in it'll be good as new."

"Frenchy's a good gunsmith."

They were entering the outskirts of Greenville. The train for Cincinnati was puffing out of the station. Its wood-burning engine was spewing clouds of smoke from the wide-mouthed stack.

Greenville was an old town as frontier towns went. Before the Revolution it had been a fort and the scene of fierce Indian fighting. Then for a hundred years it had been a sleepy backwoods village. Now it was growing fast. The coming of the Dayton and Union Railroad had brought trade and settlers.

As Annie and Coonskin Brown rode down Broadway they passed ox teams hauling long timber to a sawmill, farmers coming in with their fall wheat for the new flour mills. Saddle horses and buggies were lined up in front of the new courthouse and Fitts Tavern. Charlie Katzenberger's wagon was picking up a load of supplies at the station for his general store.

Annie left her gun with Frenchy La Motte, the gunsmith and fur trader. She parted from Coonskin Brown there, and rode on to Will Pierson's blacksmith shop. She loved to watch the blacksmith work.

Will tied her roan to a ring. He took a horseshoe in a pair of tongs and thrust it into the hot coals in the square brick forge. Then he went to the huge bellows that was stuck into the chimney. It took a strong man to work it, and Will was strong. He pushed the great handles back and forth. The coals in the forge glowed brightly.

When the shoe was cherry red, Will took it out. The hammer clanged on the anvil and the sparks flew as he held the shoe in his tongs and shaped it to fit. He plunged it into a tub of water that hissed and steamed. As Will tried the shoe on the roan, the smell of scorched hoof wrinkled Annie's nose.

It all fascinated the girl—the big ox-sling in the corner where they shod oxen, the huge wagon wheels waiting to be re-tired. The tools, the shoes, the bar-iron that lined the walls. The mixed smells of horses, cinders, leather, and hot metal.

The open back door looked out on a wide,

When the shoe was cherry red, Will took it out

swampy meadow, deep with rank grass. On the far side Annie saw a big buck feeding. She pointed it out to Will.

"Too bad you haven't got your gun," he said.

"Left it at Frenchy's," she told him. "Besides I'd rather watch that deer than kill it."

Will painted the roan's hoofs with neat's-foot oil as a finishing touch.

"Is it all right if I pay you with game?" Annie asked.

"Sure. Game's a treat to me. Don't get a chance to hunt, myself."

Annie reached into her basket and brought out a plump partridge, neatly wrapped in wet swamp grass to keep it fresh.

"That's a nice one, Annie," Will told her. "You ought to be able to make money selling birds like that."

"Who'd buy them?" Annie asked.

"Don't know. Must be someone."

Annie led the roan over to Frenchy La Motte's and tied him outside. Frenchy had a short, red beard and dark, darting eyes. He was a restless man, a talker. His hands were always moving.

Gun-shells, traps, saddles, lanterns, axes,

[*91*]

anything a trapper could use lined his walls
and shelves. His gunsmith's bench, vise, and
tools were under a window. In the back were
piles of furs. The woodstove in a corner would
glow a comforting red when cold weather
came.

Charlie Katzenberger, who owned the general store, was talking to Frenchy when Annie
came in. He was tall, heavy, light-haired, with
twinkling blue eyes.

"Charlie, you know Annie Mozee? She's
little, but she's good hunter."

Friendly Charlie Katzenberger put out his
hand. "Glad to know you, Annie," he said.

Annie's hand was lost in the storekeeper's
big one as she said, "Hello, Mr. Katzenberger."

Frenchy passed Annie her gun. She tried
the hammer. It had a strong snap.

Annie leaned the rifle against the counter.
She took a big quail from the basket. It was
fat with good fall feeding.

"Can I pay you with this?" she asked as she
passed it to the gunsmith.

"It's better than money," Frenchy said.

With his quick movements, he unwrapped

"Can I pay you with this?" she asked

the bird from the swamp grass, and thrust it toward Charlie Katzenberger.

"Look!" he said. "It's shot right through the head. Annie Mozee never misses."

Katzenberger took the bird in his hand, turned it over.

"Nice," he said. He looked at Annie. "Can you get many like this?"

"Quite a few," Annie told him.

"Do you know that the big hotels in Cincinnati will pay extra for birds shot through the head? People don't break their teeth biting down on bird shot. That they like. Would you want to hunt for me? I can sell everything you'll bring in."

Annie was excited. "I'd love to. I like to hunt. I can get all kinds of game besides quail —rabbits, partridges, turkey, pigeons."

"It's a deal then."

Katzenberger put out his big hand again and they shook on it.

Frenchy was beaming.

"Good. This is fine. You may have shells, traps, Annie. Anything you want, you can charge, till you get started. A new gun maybe, even."

Annie's eyes were shining with happiness.

The September evening was cool as she rode home, thinking of her wonderful project. The stars came out white and frosty. The harvest smells that had been so warm and sweet in the morning sun, now had a tang to them.

From then on Annie spent most of her time hunting. It was ideal country for birds. Thick woods, cornfields, pastures, brushy fence rows, feed and shelter suited to many kinds of game. Almost the whole year round there was something fit for market.

"Tha'll never get schooling this way. It worries me, Annie," her mother would say.

But Grandpap Shaw was gradually losing his sight. Soon he wouldn't be able to earn any money at all. Annie felt that she had to go on working. And though she wanted to get some education, she really enjoyed what she was doing.

Mr. Katzenberger arranged for all her game to be sold to a man named Jack Frost. He ran a hotel in Cincinnati where many actors and other people in the theater stayed. Annie sent her game into Greenville with the mail, and it went eighty miles by rail from there to the big city.

To make her work more interesting, Annie

practiced all kinds of trick shooting. When a
bird rose drumming from a brush pile, she
would whirl around before pulling the trigger. She would give the birds every possible
chance to escape, and still she didn't miss. She
would try the most difficult wing shots she
could invent. She would take a run, a skip and
a jump—in short, do everything but stand on

her head. But still she brought down the birds. Her skill with a gun became known around the county. Sometimes she would enter local shooting contests, and she always won.

All her money she turned over to her mother. All the hard times Annie had been through had made her old for her age. She understood the value of money, and all her life she never liked to see it wasted.

Slowly the mortgage on the farm was paid off till at last it was clear.

"Annie, what would I ever do without thee?" her mother often asked.

By the time Annie was fifteen, the younger children could be of more help and Annie began to think seriously about her future.

One day a letter arrived from Cincinnati. It was from Lyda. It was addressed to Annie and was the first letter she had ever had from her sister, but she couldn't read it! There was a catch in her throat as she said, "Read it to me, Mother."

Her mother slit the envelope and began:

"Dear Annie,
Joe and I have been talking it over, and we want you to come and live with us here in the city. You have done more than your share in taking care of the family. We

"Read it to me, Mother"

think it is time you did something for yourself. You are fifteen and you have hardly been to school at all. You can't spend all your life walking around the woods with a gun on your shoulder. You will get like old Coonskin Brown."

Annie's mother chuckled, and Annie burst out laughing. Mrs. Shaw went on:

"There are many things a girl like you can do in a place like this. Learn to play the piano, perhaps. Or to do fancy sewing. You can meet all kinds of interesting people and learn how to behave socially."

"My, my," Annie mocked. "How Lyda has come on!"

"Annie, I have always had a feeling about you—that there was something to you beyond the rest of us. Everything you do has more life to it. Like making paper dolls when we were little, for instance. Yours always seemed more alive. Please come. I'm sure that you will be glad all your life. I know you love the country and the woods and hunting and all that. But Annie, you were meant for bigger things. Have Mother write when you are coming, and we will meet the train.

Love,
Lyda"

Annie sat down with a lump in her throat. A sudden wave of homesickness had come over her.

"Mother," she said, "I don't want to leave

[*99*]

Darke County. I don't want to leave you and the other children and Grandpap Shaw. This is my home and I love it here. I like the country. I don't want to live in a city all cooped up. I'd be miserable."

Grandpap Shaw had come in from putting the horse away. He had been listening in the doorway.

"We don't want you to go any more than you want to, Annie," he said. "But it's the best thing for you."

Grandpap had once lived in Cincinnati himself. He began to tell of all the wonders there. The theaters. The fine white paddle-wheel steamers. The horsecars, the music. All the fine people she would meet.

"And shooting clubs, Annie. There's lots of them. The town is full of Germans and they love to shoot."

"Thee can always come home, Annie," her mother said. "This will always be thy home to come back to. But never to hold thee down."

When John and Hulda and Emily came in from school, they whooped with joy at the news. They knew it would make more work for them, since they would have to do their sister's chores. But they were glad for Annie. And some day it would be their turn to go to the city.

That night Annie went out to say good-by to the roan horse. Afterwards she stood by the stable door, breathing in the pleasant farm smells. The full harvest moon shone over the rows of shocked corn in the field. A cowbell tinkled in the pasture. A flurry of breeze sent red leaves swirling from a swamp maple. Off in the woods a fox barked. From far away came the crack of a rifle. Someone was hunting in the moonlight.

Annie went in and climbed into bed. But it was a long time before she went to sleep.

CHAPTER TEN

Shooter's Hill

LYDA and Joe Stein lived in a hilly section in the northwest part of Cincinnati. That part of the city was called Fairmount. On top of the hill above their house was a big German shooting club called *Schuetzenbuckel*.

In Annie's time, shooting was as much the national sport as baseball is today. On holidays, instead of going to baseball games, people went to shooting matches. Great shots were heroes then, as great baseball players are now.

Almost every household had guns, and almost every boy was brought up to use one. Most of the people in America lived in the country. Boys were taught to shoot game to help supply food for their families, and many of them shot well. But for a girl to be an expert hunter and a sure-shot, like Annie Moses, was something special!

From the part of the hill where the Steins lived they could see east to the Ohio River. Lyda pointed out to Annie the different parts of town. "Over there near the curve of the river is a nice section, called Hyde Park and Oakley. We were thinking of moving there when we took this house."

"Oakley . . ." Annie repeated. "Oakley—that's a nice name."

Joe Stein touched her arm. "Come on, Annie, we want to show you the town," he said.

They took a horsecar to Vine Street, and got off in a glare of bright lights. The street was alive with people. Oyster peddlers and hot-corn men blew their shrill whistles. Lights and music streamed from hotels, theaters, arcades, and concert halls. Annie and the Steins passed the Coliseum—a big hall with a stage at one end. Food was sold in this hall, and people could eat while they watched performers on the stage. Annie wanted to stop and look in, but in the distance she heard the sound of shooting.

"It's a German shooting club," Joe explained.

"Could we go watch them?" Annie asked.

"No. It's private. But if you want to shoot, come on. We'll go to Charlie Stuttleberg's shooting gallery."

No one was at the gun counter in front of the targets as they entered. Charlie himself

was reading a newspaper under a gas flare.

Joe took first try. "Once I could shoot," he said.

He shot six bullets, and knocked over two flat metal rabbits.

"Try it, Annie," Lyda said. "Maybe you can win a prize."

"It's free if you hit the bell five times," Charlie said without looking up.

"Bell?" Annie asked. "I don't see any."

"The bell in the bull's eye," Joe told her.

There was a white target with black rings and a black hole in the center. The bell was behind that.

Annie picked up the gun. She pumped in a shell, sighted, and shot.

Bong! She hit the target dead center. She tried it again. *Bong!* Dead center again. She pulled the trigger three more times as fast as she could. The bell rang each time.

Stuttleberg had put down his paper and was watching her. He picked up another loaded gun and passed it to Annie.

"Try again with this gun," he said. "It won't cost you a cent."

A row of make-believe ducks were moving along across the target board. Annie hefted the new gun, cuddled the stock to her cheek. She pulled the trigger lightly six times. Six ducks in a row dropped.

"I can't believe it!" The shooting-gallery owner was wide-eyed.

"She's used to shooting birds in the country," Joe explained.

Stuttleberg passed Annie another gun. "Do you mind trying just one more gun?" he asked.

"Of course not. It's fun," Annie said.

This time she rang the bell three times. Then she pointed the gun at a row of moving rabbits. She knocked two down at the ends and one in the middle.

"It must be true," Stuttleberg said with wonder in his voice. "Shooting like that just can't be only luck."

Annie looked pleased. "I'm market hunter for Mr. Frost's Bevis House," she said. "I get lots of practice."

"The Bevis House, eh? That's where Frank Butler's staying. Have you heard of him?"

Annie shook her head.

"Well, he and a man named Graham have a shooting act at the Coliseum. Frank's one of the best shots in the United States, but I wouldn't be surprised if you could beat him."

Charlie Stuttleberg reached for his hat. "Let's go to the Bevis House, folks," he said. "I want to introduce Jack Frost to this little lady. It's about time he met his game hunter."

A little later they were in the lobby of the Bevis House. The tall man who owned the hotel spied Stuttleberg and came over.

"Jack," the shooting-gallery man said, "meet Annie Moses, your hunter."

Jack Frost put out his hand. He looked down into Annie's clear gray eyes. "So you're the little girl I've heard so much about," he said. "I'm not surprised. You have the eyes for shooting. Charlie, every bird she sends in here is shot through the head."

"I believe it—after what she did at my shooting gallery. I think she can outshoot Frank Butler. Jack, I'd like to see a match between those two!"

Mr. Frost looked doubtful. "Frank would never shoot against a little girl," he said.

"Don't tell him who his opponent will be," suggested Stuttleberg. "See what you can do to arrange it."

"Are you willing, young lady?" Frost asked Annie.

Annie looked at Joe and Lyda questioningly. "It's up to you," Joe said. "I don't know any reason why you shouldn't try it if you want to."

"I do," Annie said almost breathlessly. Somehow this seemed the most important thing that had ever happened to her.

That night she dreamed of falling ducks in a shooting gallery and one that stood up and wouldn't fall over no matter how many times she hit it. She hoped this wasn't a bad omen.

Next day Joe stopped at the Bevis House. When he got home Annie could hardly wait for the news.

"What happened?" she asked eagerly. "I don't suppose Frank Butler will—"

"Yes, he will," Joe interrupted. "Frost told him he wanted him to shoot against someone from upcountry. Butler asked if it was any one of three goods shots he knew about, and when Frost told him it wasn't, he didn't press. Just said, "I'm always glad to take part in a match.""

"When is the match going to be?" Lyda asked.

"Thanksgiving day at *Schuetzenbuckel*—Shooter's Hill," Joe said.

The shooting club had once been a Baptist school. It was a big building with wide porches. There was a dining room with tables outside where people could sit and watch the shooting. There was a band that played between the matches.

The band was playing when Joe and Lyda and Annie arrived on the afternoon of the match. It was a sparkling day. An American flag was flying from the flagpole on top of the clubhouse. Red and yellow leaves were drift-

[*109*]

ing from the maple trees in the light breeze. Annie looked up the valley toward home, and wondered what the people in North Star would think of her now.

A crowd had already gathered. Annie picked out Mr. Frost. Standing beside him was a tall man with a shotgun in the crook of his elbow. He wore a belted hunting jacket and a soft green hat with a feather sticking jauntily out of the band. As they came close she saw that he had a brown mustache and red cheeks. She wondered for a moment how she could ever beat such a wonderful-looking man.

Jack Frost made the introductions.

"Frank, I want you to meet Lyda and Joe Stein—and the little girl is Annie Moses."

"I'm very glad to know you," Frank said, shaking hands all around.

Annie had brought her father's old Kentucky rifle with her to Cincinnati. She had polished the old gun up for the day, but Joe Stein was carrying it.

Frank Butler said, "I assume it's Mr. Stein that I'm to shoot against."

Jack Frost chuckled. He'd been looking forward to this surprise.

"Oh, no," he said, "it's Annie."

[*110*]

"I'm very glad to know you," Frank said

Frank Butler looked down with twinkling blue eyes at the little girl. Annie was as tall as she'd ever be, but she was just under five feet. And she weighed less than a hundred pounds. She wore a new pink gingham dress which she had made, and a sunbonnet to match. Her chestnut hair was hanging down her back in two pigtails. They were tied at the ends with narrow pink ribbon. Her blue-gray eyes were alive with excitement.

"This is surely a surprise!" Frank said. He turned reproachfully to Jack Frost. "Jack, you shouldn't have done this to me. I'll be run out of town if I beat this child."

"Don't worry," Jack Frost told him. "If I thought you could beat her, I wouldn't have made the match."

Frank Butler glanced at the long rifle in Joe's hand. He turned to Annie. "I guess you didn't bring a gun," he said. "The club can supply one."

Annie took the rifle from Joe. She cuddled it under her arm like a well-loved old friend.

"I'm going to use this," she told Butler. "I'm used to it. I've hardly ever used a shotgun."

"Well, it gives me all the better chance to win," Butler said with a smile.

The referee called to them to get ready. They were to use clay pigeons for targets. These were released from a trap by a spring. They would fly out in whatever direction the man who ran the trap wanted them to. He would always try to fool the shooters.

Frank Butler had first shot.

"Pull!" he shouted when he was ready.

The man pulled the lever. The clay disc rose up in an arc. Frank's shotgun blared. The disc burst into pieces.

Annie stood there stiff. Suddenly she was terrified. Her legs started to tremble. She glanced at the crowd. The rules were that the shooter had to call "pull" before starting to raise the gun. Annie tried, but the word stuck in her throat. She couldn't speak. The crowd was dead quiet while she waited.

Annie wanted to run away, to sink into the ground. Then suddenly she was in the Darke County woods. A partridge drummed and rose from a thicket. She remembered what to do. Just swing with the bird. Don't sight. When it feels right, squeeze the trigger.

Now she felt all right.

"*Pull!*" she said. Her voice was firm.

The bird arced up.

"*Dead,*" the referee noted without feeling.

They were each to shoot at twenty-five clay pigeons.

"*Pull . . . Dead.*"

"*Pull . . . Dead.*"

"*Pull . . . Dead.*"

[*114*]

It became a rhythm. A sing-song—even though Annie had to load her old rifle between each shot. A roar and a stirring came from the crowd. Annie didn't hear them.

Forty-eight birds flew from the trap without a miss.

The forty-ninth shot was Frank's.

"Pull . . . Miss!" The disc had shattered and dropped to earth—but out of bounds.

"Pull . . . Dead!"

Annie had won her match. A tremendous shout and a torrent of hand-clapping rose from the crowds on the porch and on the ground.

Frank Butler turned to Annie, beaming. There was a smile on the big Irishman's face as wide as the sun. He seemed very glad that Annie had won.

"Great work, Missie," he said, clasping her hand.

"Thanks, Jimmy," she said.

In her confusion and excitement Annie had got his name mixed up. But from then on they were always Missie and Jimmy to each other.

CHAPTER ELEVEN

Butler & Oakley

LIGHTS, life, and music flooded the city, and joy filled the heart of Annie Moses. Frank Butler had given her tickets to his show at the Coliseum.

Annie and Joe and Lyda had come down in the crisp fall evening to the big building at the corner of Twelfth Street and Vine.

Annie's blood flowed fast as they rubbed shoulders with the crowd of people going in. She edged over toward the wall and looked at the pictures of the performers. There were acrobats, comedians, singers, and jugglers. Annie's heart skipped a beat when she saw that Frank Butler's picture was the biggest of them all.

[*117*]

A waiter led Annie, Joe, and Lyda to a well-placed table where they had a good view of the stage.

"I guess Frank Butler must have fixed things up for us," Joe said.

As the waiter held her chair for her, Annie felt very important.

On the table was a menu, and a program which listed the acts. Annie stared at the big words for a little while, but could make nothing of them. Such words as *"Wienerschnitzel"* only made her gulp.

She asked Joe to read the menu to her, and then the list of acts. By the time they had ordered their food the curtain on the stage was going up.

Annie was thrilled by act after act. The good food, the music added to the fun. She joined heartily in the hand-clapping. But all the time she was waiting for Frank Butler's trick shooting act.

At last it came. Butler and his partner, Graham, came on to a burst of applause. With them was a white poodle that trotted to the back of the stage and sat down.

Annie edged forward in her seat, watching the two marksmen. One man held objects

while the other shot at them. They took turns.
This was something Annie could understand.
When Frank split a card held edgewise toward
him, she clapped hard.

At last the white poodle came forward, and
sat down. Billy Graham set an apple on its
head. The dog balanced it solemnly.

Then Frank, at the other side of the stage,
took quick aim. He pulled the trigger. The

[*119*]

apple fell apart. The dog flicked his head and caught a piece of the apple in his teeth. Then he took it to the back of the stage, lay down, and ate it.

Annie burst into laughter, and the whole audience joined her.

When the act was over, a waiter brought Joe Stein a message from Frank, asking them all to come backstage. This was quite an honor. They followed the waiter up some stairs and threaded their way through the jumble of scenery, ropes, and scaffolding. Behind all this was a row of dressing rooms.

The waiter knocked on the door of one. Frank opened it, and welcomed them in. He introduced them to Billy Graham and to the white poodle, George, who came solemnly forward to Annie and presented a paw to be shaken.

Frank said, smiling, "You must have a way with dogs, Missie. Generally George doesn't like women. I have to watch him or he'll bite them."

Annie didn't know whether or not Frank was joking. She had seen that he had a great sense of humor. One thing that made the Butler and Graham act so popular was the steady stream of funny remarks and jokes that went along with the shooting.

Before Annie and the Steins left, Frank invited them for another night. Annie went home in a daze. She could hardly wait for that night to come. When it did, she found that some of the acts had been changed. She enjoyed them all, but for her the Butler and Graham shooting act was best.

This time George, the poodle, caught the bit of apple when it was shot from his head, as usual. But instead of going back to his corner, George jumped over the footlights. He trotted straight to Annie and put his head on her lap. Then he looked up at her as though to say, "Hello, Friend. I was afraid you weren't coming back."

Frank came after him, laughing, and making a joke of the whole thing. He pretended it was part of the act.

But the third time Annie came to the Coliseum George jumped off the stage and ran to her without even stopping to do his trick. That was too much. Joe Stein apologized and asked Frank Butler to come home with them for dinner.

After that Frank often visited the Steins. In

time he and Annie became close friends, and on June 22nd, 1876, they were married.

Annie felt that now she had a real opportunity to get on with her schooling. With Frank's help, she began to study hard. She kept it up till she was better educated than many people who go to regular schools. But her chief interest was always shooting. Week after week she watched Frank and Billy perform on the stage, and her interest in their work never failed.

One morning Billy Graham was ill—too ill to do his part in the act.

"Billy can't go on, and I can't do the act without him," Frank told Annie that afternoon. "We should have had an understudy."

Annie shook her long chestnut curls over her shoulders.

"I'll take his part, Jimmy," she said quietly.

Frank looked at her, startled.

"It's good of you to offer, Missie," he said. "But you can't do it. You've never practiced any of those trick shots, and you have no costume. No, it won't do."

"Listen, Jimmy," Annie said, "I've watched that act till I know it by heart. And you know I can hit what I point at. That's really all that's needed. I can go on without a costume. You can say I'm taking Billy's place. It won't hurt for one night."

Frank looked down, thinking. "We've sold every seat in the Coliseum," he said. "We'd have to give back all the money. Perhaps—if you'd be object holder—just hold the targets while I shoot at them—it would work. Would you do that?"

"I don't know why I shouldn't do more than that," Annie protested. "I don't mind holding

objects. But I'll trade shot for shot with you
—just the same as if I were Billy. You hold
while I shoot, and I'll hold while you shoot."

"Is that the only way you'll do it?" Frank
asked.

"That's the only way," Annie said firmly.

Frank paced up and down the floor. Finally
he made up his mind.

"By gum," he said, "we'll try it!"

He was all enthusiasm now that it was decided. He patted Annie on the shoulder.

"You know, Missie, you're a great little girl.
But we haven't even time for a rehearsal."

Annie flashed him her wide smile. "There's
nothing to do but shoot, is there?"

They went down to the theater and broke
the news to the manager. He agreed to make
an announcement to the audience, and introduce Annie.

"What name do you want to use?" he asked.

"Why, Mrs. Frank Butler."

"But husband-and-wife acts aren't very
popular," he said. "I think it would be better
if you called yourself something else."

Annie thought a minute. Suddenly a name
popped into her head. *Oakley*. She remembered the fine view from Lyda's house on

Fairmount, and how she had liked the name when Lyda had pointed out that section of town. She said the word aloud—"Oakley. Do you like that?"

The manager said, "Annie Oakley. Yes. I like it. Perfect. It's a good name."

When it was time for the act to go on, the manager made the announcement.

"We are sorry to have to announce," he said, "that Billy Graham has been taken ill suddenly, and cannot shoot today. However," he went on, "we have been able to get the services of an expert shot. This person is not a professional. But we believe she can shoot like one. Ladies and gentlemen, let me introduce Frank Butler and—*Annie Oakley.*"

The tall Irishman and the little girl from Darke County stepped from the wings. Annie had left her wavy hair hanging about her shoulders. She looked so tiny with the rifle cuddled under her right arm that people began to applaud. Annie lifted the rifle over her head and waved it. Then she took up her position for her first shot.

She had only to knock a cork from the bottom of a glass that Frank held upside down. It wasn't difficult. But Annie missed! She wasn't used to the light.

The audience was quiet.

Quickly, Annie felt what was wrong. The second shot went true, and every shot after that.

When she and Frank had finished, the crowd called them back time after time. At last Frank sent Annie out alone on the stage and only that quieted the audience. The people not only were amazed at her shooting. They admired the pluck of a girl who could hold a dime steady until it was shot from her fingers.

The next morning Annie was buying material for costumes. The doctor had said that Billy Graham would never be able to play again. From then on the team was called "Butler & Oakley."

From the start it was more popular than the old team. Frank taught Annie every trick he knew. He told her, *"Practice, practice, practice. And believe in yourself."* That Annie did with all her heart and soul. Frank's rule became her motto for the rest of her life. She always lived up to it.

Up and down the land they traveled till the team of Butler & Oakley was the top shooting act in the country. Gradually Annie became the leading member of the team.

CHAPTER TWELVE

The "Bill Show"

IT WAS a soft spring evening at the close of a long season. Annie and Frank were in their gaslit dressing room. Frank was admiringly watching Annie pack her costumes. She had made them herself, and covered them with fine embroidery. No matter how tired she was, she always took perfect care of them.

Frank looked at his watch.

"Come on, Missie," he teased. "The train leaves for Darke County in an hour. Throw 'em in the trunk for once, and let's go."

"Yes? And spend hours ironing them when I get home?" Annie answered tartly.

Frank turned serious. "Don't you ever get tired of this life, Missie? Hot, dusty trains.

She had made them herself

Poor hotels, bad beds, tasteless food. Practicing all the time to keep the act fresh?"

"It's hard work, Jimmy," Annie said. "But it's lots of fun. Besides, we're saving money, and some day we'll be able to retire, to live on the farm and—"

A big man loomed in the door of their dressing room. He had a grizzled beard and his bald head shone under the gaslights as he lifted his hat.

"Pardon me," he said. "I'm Lewis Sells, of Sells Brothers' Circus. I like your act—"

"Thank you," Annie said. Frank asked him to come in and sit down. Sells sat down on a rifle box and looked at Annie.

"I wonder if you could shoot from the back of a horse the way you shoot on the stage?" he asked.

"I don't know," Annie told him. "I've ridden around a farm ever since I can remember. Maybe I could learn."

"I think you could," Sells said. "Miss Oakley, I believe you're the kind of girl who can learn almost anything she puts her mind to."

"You're right about that," Frank told him.

"Good," said Sells. "Will you come with my circus?"

He named a salary that was more than they could make in vaudeville.

They knew that the Sells Brothers' Circus was one of the best and biggest. If they took this job they would have a chance to work all summer, which vaudeville actors could not do. They could also add to their little store of savings.

Annie and Frank looked at each other a minute.

Then Annie nodded.

"We'll take your offer," Frank said like a flash.

Soon they had started a life under canvas and on show trains that would last for many years.

In a way it was a hard life. But it was fun. The stir and bustle when the circus moved from town to town. The excitement of being with animals—elephants, lions, tigers, and the other beasts, large and small. The roars of an approving audience. And the colorful parades before each show.

They especially liked the fact that show people are the most friendly in the world. To Annie and Frank the show was like a home on the road.

Frank had never seen Annie ride before. Even he was amazed at her ability. With her fine rhythm and timing she took naturally to a horse's back.

It wasn't long before she was riding standing up on a galloping white circus horse, and shooting balls thrown by Frank, who rode beside her.

Fall came. It was time for the circus to go into winter quarters. Annie and Frank were wondering whether to go back on the stage or spend a restful winter with Annie's mother at North Star. Lewis Sells knocked on the pole of their tent, and came in with a newspaper in his hand.

"Look at this," he said, pointing to a headline that read:

WORLD'S INDUSTRIAL AND COTTON
EXPOSITION IN NEW ORLEANS
THE BIGGEST EXHIBIT, THE BIGGEST
BUILDING, THE BIGGEST INDUS-
TRIAL EVENT IN THE WORLD'S
HISTORY

The item went on to explain that New Orleans was celebrating the one hundredth anniversary of the export of Louisiana cotton. It was to be a mammoth show. Railroads and

[*133*]

steamboats were advertising special rates and excursions. People were expected to pour in hordes from all over the world into the Crescent City.

"This is the best chance for a circus to make a fortune that I've ever seen," Sells said. He was bursting with joy. "I want to hire grounds before anyone gets ahead of me. Will you go?"

Again Butler & Oakley had a quick decision to make. Annie thought wistfully of the Ohio cornfields on a blue-and-gold October morning. She thought of her mother, and of restful nights in the log cabin. It was bigger now. A frame kitchen and dining room had been added with money that Annie had sent home. It would be nice. But the winter in New Orleans sounded like a great chance.

Annie sighed and gave up the dream. Again she nodded to Frank.

"We'll go," he told the circus manager.

When the New Orleans World's Fair opened in December, Sells Brothers had set up their tent in a field near the river. It was a tiny dot compared to the Fair Building. That had thirty-three acres under one roof.

And another show was in town in hopes of making money from the Fair crowds. Their great publicity man, Major John Burke, had plastered the city with their announcements. Shooting acts were one of the main features. So Annie and Frank read their posters and billboards with interest.

BUFFALO BILL'S ROCKY MOUNTAIN AND PRAIRIE EXHIBITION

The grassy sward our carpet,
Heaven's azure canopy our canvas.
A Year's Visit West in Three Hours

A company of recognized historical scouts, led by America's most renowned Frontiersman, monarch among celebrities of the plains, late Chief of Scouts, U. S. Army,

HON. W. F. CODY
BUFFALO BILL

Major Frank North, Commander, U. S. Indian Scouts, Captain David C. Payne, "The Oklahoma Raider," Captain A. H. Bogardus, magic manipulator of the shotgun, for 13 years Recognized Champion of the World, and his four marksman sons,

EUGENE BOGARDUS
EDWARD BOGARDUS
HENRY BOGARDUS
PETER BOGARDUS

With three great shows in town, everyone hoped that the sun would shine on Crescent City. Instead it rained. It poured. It was cloudy, muggy, and hot. Then it rained some

[*135*]

more. The show grounds were nothing but deep mud, soggy canvas, and sad performers.

It rained for forty-four days and no one made any money. Sells' Circus had stopped paying their people. For the team of Butler & Oakley this was bad.

One day Frank and Annie were sitting in their tent. They were tired of rain beating on the roof and the smell of mildewed canvas. Frank was playing cards with himself, and Annie was embroidering a fancy design on one of her costumes. Her quick fingers moved faster and faster. A frown settled on her forehead.

Suddenly she put down her work.

"Jimmy," she said, "let's go over and talk to the Buffalo Bill people."

"And break our contract here?" Frank asked.

"I just said 'talk,' " Annie reminded him. "Besides, the contract was broken when Sells stopped paying us."

"All right," Frank said, "it's better than sitting here doing nothing."

Before long they were talking with Major Burke, who told them that the Buffalo Bill show was as badly off as Sells Brothers' Circus.

"Bogardus and his sons have quit, and we need a shooting act, but we can't afford to pay people like you," Burke said.

Annie thought quickly.

"Give us a three-day trial," she suggested. "We'll work on those days for nothing. Then you can decide whether you can afford to pay what we ask."

"Fair enough," Burke agreed. "But we're breaking up here now and you'll have to wait until next spring. We're opening up then in Louisville, Kentucky, under the new name of *Buffalo Bill's Wild West*. Meet us there and we'll see what happens."

[*137*]

CHAPTER THIRTEEN

The Happy Family

THE TRUNKS and the gun case marked *Butler & Oakley* were dropped on the station platform at Louisville, Kentucky, on April 23rd, 1885. The owners of the trunks and their snow-white poodle, George, reached the platform at the same time. George was getting quite old, but he was still a brave trouper.

As soon as they were settled in a hotel room Frank went downstairs and bought a copy of the *Louisville Courier Journal*. He started turning the pages. Suddenly he folded it over and passed it to Annie.

"Look at this," he said.

There was a big picture of cowboys, Indians, wigwams, and a wagon train on a wide prairie. Under it was the announcement:

THE HAPPY FAMILY

Louisville Base Ball Park, three afternoons only,
April 24, 25, & 26, reconstructed, enlarged, improved,

the only original

BUFFALO BILL'S
WILD WEST

America's National Entertainment

including two hundred Indians, Scouts, Cowboys, Mexicans, Herds of Buffalo, Elk, Steers, Ponies, etc. One hundred and twenty days at the New Orleans Exposition. Street Parade Friday morning.

"Two hundred performers. Quite a show this year," Frank said.

It seemed big to Annie and Frank then. But later there were close to eight hundred people working with the show. That is counting canvasmen, ticket takers, kitchen help, and so on.

Next morning Annie and Frank took a cab to the ball park. The Indian lodges had been set up on the show grounds. So had the other tents. But except for a man in a white apron who was leaning in the mess-tent door, not a soul was in sight. Buffalo and elk chewed their cuds in their own corral. The buckers, looking innocent as angels, lazed in the sun.

But not a painted Indian war horse, not a cowpony was there.

[*139*]

"They must all be out in the parade," Frank guessed.

"Good. That gives us a chance to practice. I'm pretty rusty," Annie told him.

Frank got out the folding gun table and a portable trap.

Annie picked up her gun and sighted. For once she was not in costume. The clothes were stiff in the shoulder.

"Pull!" she ordered.

The clay pigeon flew up. A clean miss.

She tried again. Another miss.

The man at the mess tent laughed. "Get a cannon!" he shouted.

"We'll try it again tomorrow," Frank said. "The light's wrong. Your clothes are wrong. You're tired from the trip."

"Nonsense," Annie said impatiently. "We've had lots worse conditions than this— Try once more. Pull!"

This time the disc burst in the air.

"The balls," Annie said. Frank got them from their box.

He threw up one. Annie hit it. He tossed two. She got them both before they hit the ground. Three. The same story.

Now things were going well.

She called to the poodle. "Up, George."

She placed George on her gun table, put a stone on his head, and sent it flying with one shot. Then she spied a bicycle leaning against one of the tents. She hopped on and went racing around the ball park. She didn't use the handlebars, but steered by balance. And as

she raced around she shot balls to bits as fast as Frank could throw them into the air.

Finally she fell off the bicycle into Frank's arms, laughing wildly.

"Oh, Jimmy!" she said when she could stop. "For a minute I was afraid I couldn't do it. I was afraid I'd never hit anything again."

A voice sounded behind them. Annie straightened up and looked around. A slender man in striped trousers and a cutaway coat was standing there. His eyes were alight with enthusiasm.

"Great!" he said, putting out his hand to Annie. "Best shooting I ever saw."

He shook hands with Frank. "I'm Nate Salsbury," he said. "Buffalo Bill's partner. And you must be Butler & Oakley. We've been expecting you. Burke told me about you. But he didn't lead me to expect anything quite so marvelous. Now, how about some pictures—I want to get an order for posters off right away."

"I haven't anything recent. With the circus—" Annie began.

"Never mind. We'll get you downtown this afternoon. Some tin-type pictures will be the thing. Have you costumes ready? Can you go on this afternoon?"

And so it was settled. There was no mention of the three-day trial. There was never any mention of a contract. From then on Butler & Oakley were part of the family—of Buffalo Bill's Wild West. They hadn't been hired. They'd been adopted.

Before they could talk any more, they heard a horse neigh. Then the rumble of hoofs. The clunk and clatter of wagon wheels. The snap of a whip. The shouts of teamsters.

"Yowee! . . . Yowee! . . . Yip Yip Yaow! Y-a-a-a- H-o-o-o!"

A bunch of cowboys drove a herd of wild cattle into a corral. Horns rattling, they went through in a cloud of dust. Indians filled the air with war whoops. Feathered headdresses streamed down their backs. Dressed in all the finery of their best beaded buckskin, they came galloping in on their brightly splotched war horses. They slipped to the ground, stripped off their saddles, and headed for their tepees.

A pony express rider came along with his special mail saddle. Next came the Deadwood Stage Coach driven by John Y. Nelson. His long beard floated over his shoulder in the spring breeze. His skilled fingers handled the reins over six shiny black mules. Old John was in charge of the Indian camp. He was married to the daughter of an Oglala Sioux chief. His Indian name was *Cha-sha-na-po-ge-o*. It meant "Red Willow Fill the Pipe." Old John preferred to be called by it. Two of his many handsome children sat on the seat of the stagecoach beside him.

Next came a train of pack mules. Behind that lumbered the big ox-drawn prairie schooner.

Suddenly from behind the prairie schooner there appeared a beautiful, tall white horse. Riding him was the handsomest man Annie had ever seen. He was almost six feet tall, broad-shouldered, deep-chested, straight as an arrow. His long hair fell over his shoulders in waves. His mustaches curved. A neatly trimmed Vandyke beard came to a point on his chin.

He lifted the white horse to a hand gallop and rode toward them. The rhythm between horse and rider was so perfect that they seemed like one lovely animal.

The tall man swept off his wide sombrero as he stepped down from his horse before them.

Nate Salsbury made the introduction.

Riding the white horse was the handsomest man
Annie had ever seen

"Colonel, I want you to meet Annie Oakley and Frank Butler. My friends, this is Buffalo Bill."

"Welcome to the Wild West," Cody said as he shook hands.

And then a bugle blew brightly from the mess tent. There was a rush from all over the lot. Indians, cowboys, Mexican fancy ropers quickly shed their race or nationality under the pangs of hunger.

Colonel Cody and Nate Salsbury with Butler and Oakley moved forward at a slower pace. As they entered the mess tent everyone looked up. Buffalo Bill raised his hand for silence. Then his strong voice boomed out.

"Boys," he said. "This little missie here is Miss Annie Oakley. She's come to be the only woman sure-shot with our show. I want you to welcome and protect her. The gentleman is her husband and shootin' partner, Frank Butler . . . I reckon he can take care of himself."

With a laugh everyone turned back to his food. Annie noticed there was plenty of it, and it looked and smelled good. As she learned later, the Buffalo Bill family was always the best fed outfit on the road.

They sat down at one of the long tables and ate a good meal.

An hour later Annie was sitting on a paint pony, in a Western stock saddle. Her heart was beating like a rabbit's. She heard Frank Richmond, the announcer's, voice. "Ladies and gentlemen: The Honorable William F. Cody and Nathan Salsbury present the foremost woman marksman in the world, in an exhibition of skill with the rifle, shotgun, and pistol —the little girl of the Western plains—Annie Oakley!"

Annie put spurs to her pony and came around the barrier at a high lope. Ahead of her a cowboy paced her to a slower ride. He began to toss balls in the air. She raised her rifle to her shoulder. The balls burst as fast as he could throw them. How familiar it all was! But the surroundings were the most thrilling Annie had ever worked in.

Through her routine she went on horseback and foot. Frank was waiting for her, juggling balls in the air. As she dismounted he tossed up four balls. Annie ran and jumped over her gun table, picked up a gun. Two glass balls disappeared. She picked up another. The other two balls blew apart. Next came the mirror trick, using a polished knife blade for a mirror.

Frank stood quite a way behind her. He held up an ace of spades. Annie held her gun pointed back over her shoulder. She held the knife blade in front of her, sighted in it. She pulled the trigger. The gun barked. A hole appeared where the spade had been in the center of the card.

As the crowd burst into cheers, Annie swung aboard the paint pony, and touched him with the spur. The beat of his hoofs echoed off the arena wall.

Back by the barrier, Buffalo Bill sat in his buggy, holding in a pair of half-wild mustangs. As Annie went by he shouted, "Sharp shooting, Missie!"

A cowboy caught the pony. Annie jumped off into Frank's arms.

"Jimmy," she said, "this is it! This is what we've been working toward. Here is where our act belongs."

"I think you're right," Frank said, grinning with pride.

CHAPTER FOURTEEN

Tatanka Iyotake

No, JOHNNY! Do it this way."

Annie Oakley took the rifle from little Johnny Baker, who had just missed a clay pigeon.

"Give us another, Jimmy," she said.

Frank Butler pulled the lever of the trap. A clay disc flew out at an angle. Annie was back to it. She swung around, squeezed the trigger. The rifle barked and the disc flew apart.

"You can't take time to aim, Johnny," Annie told the boy. "Swing with the target, and when it feels right, pull."

Little Johnny Baker was Buffalo Bill's foster son. He was only about twelve years old, but he could already shoot glass balls out of the air.

Annie was teaching him the fine points that Buffalo Bill hadn't had time to teach him.

A shout went up as Annie broke the pigeon. They were surrounded by children.

That morning, June 12th, 1885, the show had arrived at Driving Park in Buffalo. Swarms of boys and girls always showed up as soon as the show reached a town. Buffalo Bill let them wander over the grounds and see everything.

They marveled at rows of beautiful horses, the herd of buffalo, the longhorn steers, the ox-drawn covered wagon, the Deadwood Stage Coach, the real cowboys. They loved to watch the speed with which the Indian squaws put up the huge painted tepees, and the Indian children with buffalo-horn headdresses.

But they usually found Annie practicing. And when her gun began to crackle, they'd leave anything else to watch her.

Now Annie, carrying her gun, jumped lightly up on a beautiful white horse that Frank was holding. Standing on its back, she began to gallop around the park.

Little Johnny Baker mounted another horse and rode around ahead of her, tossing balls in the air. She broke them all. Then she lay on her back with the horse still galloping. She didn't miss a ball.

As she slid off, children crowded around her.

A bold one asked, "Miss Oakley, how did you ever learn to do that?"

"Practice," Annie told him, smiling.

"Could I learn?" he asked.

"Perhaps. You have to believe in yourself. Practice, practice, practice, and believe in yourself. It's the only way—"

Annie broke off. Two cabs had driven into the Arena, and a strange group of people were getting out.

First came big, fat Major Burke with his long, blond mustache. Behind him was a stern-looking Indian. He had a feathered headdress that spread out on his head like a turkey tail, and flowed all the way down his back to the ground. He was broad-shouldered and stood very straight. Behind him came five other Indian braves and three squaws. They were all dressed in richly beaded buckskin.

"Who are they?" one of the children asked. It didn't take children long to have confidence in Annie Oakley's friendship.

[151]

Children crowded around her

"Sitting Bull and his people," Annie told them gravely. "Buffalo Bill has invited them to join the show, and Major Burke went all the way to Dakota to get them."

"Sitting Bull! The one who massacred General Custer and his soldiers!" one boy said in an excited voice.

"The battle of the Little Big Horn wasn't a massacre. It was a fair fight," Annie said. "Yes, Sitting Bull was one of the leaders. He is a great medicine man."

"What's his Indian name?" one child asked.

"Tatanka Iyotake," Annie told him.

Sitting Bull and his people disappeared into the tents that had been prepared for them. They had to be ready for the show soon. So did Annie.

Annie Oakley had helped bring luck to Buffalo Bill's Wild West Show. Ever since she joined it at Louisville there had been big crowds. Annie's act had always come first. Today she was to follow Sitting Bull. He was supposed to be the big feature.

When Annie Oakley mounted her horse behind the big canvas fence at the end of the Arena, there were ten thousand people in the stands. But it turned out that most of them didn't feel the same way that Annie did about Tatanka Iyotake.

John Burke was holding in a pair of Indian paint ponies hitched to a shining carriage. Beside him sat the great medicine man in his beaded buckskins and feathered headdress.

His face was daubed with war paint, and his heavy jaw seemed carved in rock.

The grand entry march was finishing. At the end of it, a group of brightly dressed Mexican ropers galloped out of the Arena.

Major Burke gave slack to the reins, and the paint ponies jumped away, as they galloped through the gate. The audience was quiet as John skillfully slowed them to a trot and brought them to a stop in the center.

The strong voice of the announcer, Frank Richmond, came clearly in the silence.

"Ladies and gentlemen, let me introduce Tatanka Iyotake, the war chief of the fighting Sioux—the one and only Sitting Bull. He is—"

At the words, "Sitting Bull," a roar grew among the crowd. Angry shouts showered down.

To this audience, though they were wrong, Tatanka Iyotake was not a brave chief who

"The one and only Sitting Bull!"

had defended his people. To them he was the man who had ambushed and murdered General George A. Custer. He was the villain who had massacred the Seventh Cavalry. He was the savage who had left not one soldier alive on the battlefield.

"Murderer! Kill him!" they yelled. "Drag him out of that buggy. Hang the savage!"

The shouts rose to a steady roar. The great medicine man's strong, black eyes swept the grandstand with scorn. Some indignity he could take. But this was too much. He stepped down from the buggy and started to walk away, limping from an old battle wound.

Major Burke thought of his long trip and his fine contract. All time and work wasted. Buffalo Bill and Nate Salsbury watched tensely from behind the barrier. Annie Oakley was mounted. Her act was next.

"Go ahead, Annie," Nate said.

Her cowboy helper heeled his pony. Swinging a bunch of glass balls on a long thong around his head, he loped into the Arena. Annie followed. She shouldered her rifle, pointed, fired. A ball blew up. Another and another went as the galloping cowboy whirled them faster and faster.

Tatanka Iyotake stopped and looked. This was shooting. Annie went on with her fabulous tricks. Finally, when she aimed backwards, sighting in a hunting-knife mirror, and shot the spade out of the middle of the ace, Sitting Bull completely forgot himself.

"Ho! Ho! Was-te! Wa-kan!" he shouted, meaning, "It is good! It is great!"

He climbed back into the buggy.

Major Burke felt like slapping Sitting Bull on the back. But he held himself in. He knew that to touch an Indian's body is to offer him the greatest insult.

Later, after the show, John Burke found Bull sitting in front of Annie's tent. He was saying over and over, *"Machin Chilla. Wan-tan-yeya. Ci-sci-la."*

The medicine man was pointing at Annie, then at himself, then at her rifle. Then he would put his arms in shooting position, trying to make her understand.

Annie, her forehead wrinkled, was trying hard.

Major Burke watched them a minute. They hadn't noticed him. He had picked up enough Indian talk with the show to know what Sitting Bull was trying to say.

He coughed. Annie looked up. "Oh, John," she said, "what *is* he trying to say?"

"Why, Missie," John told her, "you're honored. He's adoptin' you and namin' you all at once. He's sayin', 'My daughter, Little Straight Shooter, Little Sure Shot.'"

Annie's wide smile broke over her face, and she thanked the medicine man. She learned later that Tatanka Iyotake's own daughter, who had also been a fine shot, had died, and Annie was to take her place.

The name Sitting Bull had given her became her regular show name. "Little Sure Shot" was seen on billboards all over the world.

Almost any day during the four months that Sitting Bull was with the outfit, he could be found at Annie's tent. He would sit cross-legged for hours on the floor, solemnly watching her at some fine piece of embroidery or reading a book.

The rest of the season was a triumphal march. They moved on mostly by one- and two-night stands. In Canada, Sitting Bull was the hero. Annie Oakley and Buffalo Bill had to take back seats.

The only sad thing on the tour was the

death of George, the poodle. The outfit gave him a splendid funeral.

On October 11th the show closed. It had been the first successful season of the Great Wild West Show that thrilled two generations of young Americans. And Annie knew that their act was one of the reasons for its success.

She was packing away her costumes when Tatanka Iyotake came to her tent. He had in his arms a quiver and his best arrows, moccasins bright with colored beads, and the long, feathered headdress that flowed all the way down his back to the ground. He held them out to Annie.

Annie took them and thanked him. He looked up at the sky.

Bill Halsey, the interpreter, came by, and Tatanka Iyotake spoke.

"What did he say?" Annie asked.

"He says it's going to be a cold winter," Bill told her.

Tatanka turned and walked out. It was the last time Annie ever saw him. But some of the presents he brought can be seen today in the Annie Oakley Museum in Greenville, Ohio.

Sitting Bull's prophecy of a cold winter turned out to be right. But Annie didn't care.

[*159*]

He held them out to Annie

She spent it with her mother, Grandpap Shaw, and her youngest sister, Emily. Thanks to the money Annie had been able to send home, the farmhouse was much more roomy and comfortable than ever before. Now Annie's mother could have whatever she wanted. She could have had a new house. But she liked the old log cabin with its new frame additions. The old farm was a good place to come home to.

Annie was pleased that Frank was very popular with all her Darke County friends. He was a great storyteller and was always welcome by the pot-bellied stove in the country store.

One night Annie sat in their bedroom window. A full white winter moon shone like a floodlight over the cold cornfields. It outlined the bare trees in black. Annie thought back to the lonesome October night when she had sat there not wanting to leave for Cincinnati. She thought farther back to the time she had lived with the Wolves, the hunger and abuse and the hateful song about *Moses Poses*.

Quickly she turned her mind to more cheerful things. And she thought how good life had been to her ever since. Anyone else would say she had earned it.

[*161*]

CHAPTER FIFTEEN

Sleigh Ride on Broadway

THE doctor leaned over the canvas cot. The girl in fringed buckskin who lay on it was in great pain.

Frank Butler put a cool, broad hand on her hot forehead.

"How long has this been going on?" the doctor asked him.

"For days. It began in Philadelphia. The pain in her ear has been more than an ordinary person could stand. But she hasn't missed a show."

"Great girl," the doctor said.

It was hot in the tent. Staten Island, across the bay from New York City, can be fiercely hot in July.

The doctor wiped the perspiration from his face.

"The ear is inflamed, and she has a tempera-
ture. But I don't know the cause yet." He
touched Annie's shoulder. "Young lady," he
added, "no more work for you for a while. You
stay in bed."

Annie managed a smile. "Yes, sir," she said
meekly.

The doctor spoke to Frank. "Keep ice packs
on her ear. If it doesn't get better, we'll have
to lance it." He turned and left the tent.

Annie sighed. They were back again with
the Buffalo Bill Show. This was the start of the
summer season in New York. The big parade
on Broadway was to be that morning and she
had a new costume and horse trappings.

"Don't worry, Missie. I'll stay with you,"
Frank told her.

"Don't be silly," Annie burst out. "You're
needed in the parade. Someone else can get me
ice packs."

Frank knew that this was so. Unwillingly he
left her.

Through the throbbing pain, Annie heard
the troupe getting ready to board the ferry
which would carry them across the bay to Man-
hattan. The rumbling wagons, the lowing of
cattle, the blat of a baby buffalo, the neigh-

[*163*]

ing of horses. And over all the deep voice of
Buffalo Bill giving orders.

Jingling bridle chains, pounding hoofs, and
rattling wagons passed her tent and drew away.
The sounds became faint in the distance.

Annie was furious. This would be the first
show she'd ever missed. Besides, she'd been
looking forward to seeing New York City from
horseback.

Suddenly she thought, "I certainly can't
feel any worse in the saddle than I do lying on
this cot."

She sat up, her teeth clenched against the
pain. A boy was coming in with a basin of
chopped ice.

"Bring my horse," she almost shouted at
him.

"But Missie—" the lad began to protest.

"Bring my horse, I said—and quickly!" Annie was polite but firm.

The boy knew that she meant what she said.
Annie put on her fringed jacket. She snatched
the broad-brimmed hat, pinned up jauntily at
one side with a silver star.

In five minutes she was mounted. She
touched her pony with the spur and he sped
toward the ferry. The whistle blew as they approached. The gates were down. The ferry

had begun to move as Annie clattered down the slip.

"Up! Up!"

She fairly lifted the horse. They flew over the gate, and landed with a thud on the deck of the moving ferryboat.

Buffalo Bill was the first to see her.

"Annie, you go back," he roared.

"Shall I swim or row, Bill?" Annie answered saucily.

Frank, worried, came to her side.

"I'm fine, Frank," she said. "I'm better off here than lying on that measly cot."

It was a big parade. All the way from the Battery where the ferry landed, up Eighth Avenue to Forty-second Street. Then across town, down Fifth Avenue and Broadway and back to the ferry again.

Annie hardly knew what was going on around her. The shouting crowds were a blur to her. Heat beat at her from sky, streets, and walls of buildings. The sun seemed like a brass gong that clanged in her ears.

Annie gritted her teeth and clung to the saddle. At last they rode onto the ferryboat. Annie took a deep breath of the sea breeze, and toppled unconscious into Frank Butler's arms.

When she was back on her cot, the doctor

was called again. "Blood poisoning," he said, and lanced the ear.

Four days later when Frank was bathing her ear, a bug fell out. It must have been the cause of all the trouble.

Those four days were the only ones Annie missed in all the seventeen years she was with the Buffalo Bill Show.

In the fall the show moved to Madison Square Garden in New York City for the winter. The big old building on Twenty-fourth Street had once been a railroad station. P. T. Barnum, the great circus man, had made it over. It was a perfect place for the Wild West Show, which took New York by storm.

Annie had a whirl. Flowers in her dressing room; dinner with famous people. The whole town at her feet.

But Annie never lost her sense of humor.

She and Frank had an apartment in the heart of town, not far from the Garden. Annie would cook big breakfasts, which they ate as slowly as they pleased.

One bright winter morning they were sitting by the window having breakfast. There had been a heavy snowfall the night before and the streets were still white.

[*166*]

"Jimmy," Annie said suddenly, "let's go for a sleigh ride."

She jumped up from the table and led the way down to Madison Square. When they reached the Garden she led Frank to that part of the big building where the animals were kept. She walked past all the fine horses till she came to the stall of Jerry, the moose. Together, they harnessed him and hitched him to a fine, shiny sleigh. Jerry was docile as a milk cow.

But outside, the big moose began to show his independence. He spied a pushcart full of red apples. He knocked it over and started eating the fruit. The proprietor screamed and threatened. Frank plied the whip and tugged on the reins. Jerry paid no attention.

At last the frantic peddler kicked him hard on the ankle. Jerry snorted and galloped away, while Frank tossed some money to the peddler to pay for the damage. The big moose then headed for the frozen tundras of his northern home. It took six policemen to stop him.

When Frank and Annie got back, Buffalo Bill gave them a good scolding. But John Burke thought it would be a good newspaper story. As usual, he made the most of it.

CHAPTER SIXTEEN

The Jubilee Year

A HUGE WAVE hung tottering over the stern of the steamship *Nebraska*.

"Grab something!" shouted Captain Braes.

Annie Oakley grabbed the nearest thing she saw—the steering wheel.

The wave came down hard on the deck. The ship shuddered and groaned. She swerved a bit, rolled halfway over. The water poured off the decks as she recovered and began to climb the next wave.

From between decks came the bellow of an ox, the low moaning of buffalo. The pounding of hoofs as a horse pawed his manger in fright.

Captain Braes looked at Annie. Her color was high. She seemed to be having fun.

"You're a good sailor, lass," the captain told her admiringly.

"Lucky, aren't I?" Annie replied.

"I don't know if it's luck or pluck," the captain told her. "I only know it's you up here on the bridge, and all your mates sick as cats below deck. I never saw such a pale bunch of Injuns. Even the great Buffalo Bill himself made an undignified dive for the railin'. Old Man Sea makes all men equal."

Yes, Buffalo Bill's Wild West was actually on the ocean. The show had done so well in America that Buffalo Bill had decided to try his luck in Europe. John Burke was sent ahead to get things ready, and in March, 1887, people, animals, scenery, and props were loaded on the ship *Nebraska,* bound for London.

It was a stormy trip. At one point a rudder cable broke. The *Nebraska* ran in crazy circles on the sea until they could repair it. But the weather got better, and other faces besides Annie's showed on deck.

As they came near the great city of London, a tug chugged out to meet them. The cheery face of Major John Burke beamed from the deck. The tug came alongside and John swarmed up a rope ladder.

He was full of enthusiasm. "We're all set to go. Wonderful grounds at Earl's Court. I've got the town plastered with posters. All England's waiting for us to begin."

"Hope you're right, John," Nate Salsbury said.

"How can we miss? Queen Victoria's been on the throne fifty years. It's her Jubilee Year. All the top people of Europe are coming here to celebrate."

Everything had been well planned.

"This is going to be great," Annie said to Frank as they reached the show grounds. "Look at that arena."

Carpenters were pounding away busily at a roofed-in arena that would seat 30,000 people. At one end a huge backdrop of prairies and mountains looked as real as could be.

As the opening date drew closer, the English people grew more and more excited. It began to look as though 30,000 seats wouldn't be enough for all the Londoners who wanted to be at the first performance of the Bill Show.

Edward, Prince of Wales, later King of England, couldn't wait till the show opened. On May 6th, a line of shiny carriages crossed the bridge and headed for the show grounds.

Prince Edward was in the first carriage. Lords and ladies and wide-eyed children leaned from the windows of the others. Someone on the show grounds saw them coming.

Buffalo Bill's great voice boomed out. Quickly he got things ready. He led the royal party to a flag-draped box. Then into the empty arena dashed Annie Oakley on a galloping horse. A pistol lay on the tanbark. She reached from the saddle and picked it up. On the ground, Frank started tossing targets in the air. Annie knocked them down as fast as he could throw them up.

At her last shot a herd of buffalo charged in. A hundred Wild Indians on their paint ponies were hot on their heels. Their yells pierced the mild English air. The Prince rose to his feet, eyes shining. Buffalo Bill was sitting his horse near by.

"Cody, you've sent 'em!" he said to himself.

It was true. All winter long people flocked to Buffalo Bill's Wild West Show. The grounds swarmed with visitors between shows. The performers were asked into the homes of the people. Buffalo Bill was invited to join the best clubs. He became friendly with kings and princes.

[*171*]

But Annie Oakley was the favorite. Her costumes set the style for sports clothes in England that year. Society ladies organized shooting classes, and got her to teach them. She was in demand for all sorts of exhibitions and social affairs. The best gunsmith in England made a pair of beautiful rifles for her, that ever after were her pride.

That year Annie earned a thousand dollars in one week. Her years of hardship and constant practice now were counting.

One day a uniformed messenger brought a letter sealed with the Royal Arms. Queen Victoria had asked for a show to be put on for her-

self and her guests. She came in a fine carriage surrounded by mounted guards. Half the kings and queens of Europe drove up in other carriages.

The show was especially fast and furious. Prince Edward and four kings asked to ride in the Deadwood Coach. Buffalo Bill held the door for them. Utah Frank snapped his long whip. The six mules jumped into action. The old coach rumbled off swinging and swaying, while Frank shouted the drivers' song:

> *"Pound 'em on the back*
> *Let the leaders go;*
> *Never mind the weather*
> *So the wind don't blow."*

Queen Victoria thought Annie's shooting was wonderful and sent word to Annie that she would like to meet her. When Annie was taken to the royal box, the Queen said, "You are a very, very clever little girl."

The words echoed in Annie's mind. They were so familiar. Then she remembered. They were the same words her mother had said when she had brought home her first quail.

But Annie's mind came back to the present. The Queen was still speaking:

". . . I want to claim your friendship for as long as I live."

Queen Victoria meant it. For she and Annie exchanged letters for the rest of the Queen's life.

Victoria gave Annie a handsome pair of gold and mother-of-pearl opera glasses. Along with Sitting Bull's gifts, they may be seen at the Greenville Museum.

The London season was the best yet for the Bill Show. When the show returned to America Annie went home laden with honors, gifts, and medals.

CHAPTER SEVENTEEN

Home

THE little girl from Darke County had become the most famous woman in the world. With Frank Butler always by her side, she went on from adventure to adventure. She could not appear on the street without being followed by hordes of people.

At last the show went to France and opened in Paris. They had expected as good an audience as they had had in London. But on the opening day the French people met each act with stony silence. They could not understand it.

Nate Salsbury was desperate. It was not time yet for Annie to go into the arena. But Nate decided to try it. His mind made up, he suddenly stopped his restless pacing.

[*175*]

"Perhaps they can savvy shooting," he said. "It's our only chance. Go on out there and show them, Annie."

This was Annie's biggest test. Could she bring that cold-faced crowd to life? She threw her whole soul into the act. She started with the easier stunts and worked up. When she shot the flames off a turning wheel of candles, the audience began to stir. There was a rumble of voices—a few claps. The applause grew as she went from trick to trick. The little new horse which Buffalo Bill had given her was a wonder. He worked as though he knew what was at stake.

At last Annie tried something she had not done before in public. She stood twenty paces ahead of her gun stand. A cowboy tossed six balls in the air. Annie ran and jumped over the table. She picked up the three guns one after the other. With each she broke two glass balls before any of the six hit the ground.

The crowd went wild.

"Bravo! Bravo! Vive, Annie Oakley!"

Time after time they called her back. The show was saved. They played to full stands for six months. An Eastern prince wanted to buy Annie and take her home to shoot the tigers that were killing his people.

Annie jumped over the table

Everyone loved Annie Oakley. The day before they closed in Strasbourg, which was then in Germany, Frank and Annie came into their tent to find Buffalo Bill sitting at Annie's table. He got up quickly and went out.

Annie found her autograph book open. In it Bill had written:

"To the loveliest and truest little woman, both in heart and aim, in the world. Sworn to, by and before myself. W. F. Cody, Buffalo Bill, Strasburgh, 1890."

And so the years passed until at last on tour *Buffalo Bill's Wild West and Congress of Rough Riders of the World,* as the show was then called, came to Greenville, Ohio.

Annie's heart was beating hard as the long show train passed through the familiar country, and pulled into town. She knew her mother and sisters and their children would be there. It would be a great homecoming.

Before the show Annie met her relatives. She showed the wondering children all through the vast assembly. They ate in the dining tent with the company.

People had driven into Greenville from many miles around. Twenty thousand persons were on hand to watch their own Annie. Her fame had reached them from the far places. But this was the first time most of them had seen her in action.

As it came time for her act, Annie felt a strange lightness. She wondered if she were dreaming. She cuddled her gun under her arm and closed her eyes. Would she open them to find herself in some deep glen of the Darke County woods? Would she find herself still shooting birds to feed her hungry family?

She opened her eyes. If it was a dream it was very real. The tents, the smell of canvas, the noise of the crowd, the arena. If sound, sight, touch, and smell were real, this was real.

A cowboy brought her pony, she mounted, touched spur, and galloped into the arena. Never had she heard such a roar from any crowd in all her travels.

"Annie! Annie Moses! *Hiya, Annie!*"

"Annie Moses!" The name hit her like a shock. For years she had thought of herself as Annie Oakley. She *was* Annie Oakley.

But there was no time to think about that. She went through her act in her best form. Today Annie Oakley couldn't do wrong.

She finished amid a storm of applause that rocked the stands. But as she waved her hat to

[*179*]

her friends and started to go off, Frank stopped her.

A man was walking toward them from the grandstand. Under his arms was something wrapped in velvet cloth. At first Annie didn't know him. But as he came up she recognized him, Charlie Anderson, a Darke County lawyer.

The crowd grew quiet. Charlie made a short speech. A lump grew in Annie's throat as she listened to the warm tribute.

Charlie took off the velvet cloth. He held up a big silver loving cup. Annie took it, and read the inscription:

"To Miss Annie Oakley, From Old Home Friends of Greenville, Ohio. July 25th, 1900."

Annie's words of thanks were drowned out by the cheers of the crowd. Tears streamed down her cheeks as she listened. Years filed past her mind, till at last she was working for the "Wolves." She was at the hateful school.

"Moses Poses, Moses Poses!"

Why, she hadn't thought of these words for—

Suddenly something broke loose inside her. Annie Moses Oakley began to laugh with happiness.

"Of course they said that," she thought. "I do pose. I am an actress. I'm a showgirl. And that is how all these wonderful things have come into my life."

She took Frank Butler's hand in hers and held it high overhead. People in the stands threw their hats into the air with approval. She and Frank started to walk away. But the crowd spilled down into the arena and surrounded them. Little Annie Moses had come home.

[*181*]

About the Author

EDMUND COLLIER inherited the wanderlust from his sea-faring forebears, and so, at an early age, he left his strict, respectable New England home. He set out for the West where he became a cowboy for a while, and gathered material for the many stories about cowboys and western life that have since appeared in magazines. Later he became the editor and publisher of WEST MAGAZINE but now devotes all his time to writing. It was while doing research for the Signature Book, THE STORY OF BUFFALO BILL, that he became convinced that so colorful a person as Annie Oakley deserved a book of her own.

About the Artist

LEON GREGORI's illustrations are well known, having appeared in Collier's Magazine, Red Book, and many others. Mr. Gregori was born in the United States but has traveled widely in Europe and studied there. He also studied at Pratt Institute here, George Washington University, and New York University. His particular knowledge of and interest in western and theatrical subjects made him the logical choice as the artist for THE STORY OF ANNIE OAKLEY.

"Names That Made History"
ENID LaMONTE MEADOWCROFT, *Supervising Editor*

HANDSOME BOOKPLATES: *Send your name and address to* Signature Books, Grosset & Dunlap, Inc., 1107 Broadway, New York 10, N. Y., *and we will mail you, upon receipt of ten cents to pay the cost of postage and handling, a set of handsomely designed bookplates, each one different.*

CPSIA information can be obtained
at www.ICGtesting.com
Printed in the USA
BVHW051521230123
656851BV00009B/404